Basic Typing Skills

Kathleen Dulmage

 LONGMAN

12

You wish to sell a used portable typewriter, Hermes 3000, manual, purchased new in 1975 for £275, perfect condition, elite type, price £75.

a *Prepare a classified advertisement including your telephone number and the instruction to call after 6 pm. The cost to you will be 20p per word so be brief but include the relevant information.*
b *Type a notice to place on the bulletin board advertising the typewriter. Use a variety of display techniques.*

13

Write to a nearby primary school to invite any interested teachers to a reception for author Lily Weston whose books include Dexter Bear, Spider on the Run, and Hello, Up There. The reception will be in the company board room on Friday 15 June from 3-5. Neil Carson, Public Relations Director of Universal Books will sign it.

14

Prepare a table and centre it horizontally & vertically showing staff promotions. Don Hall was promoted from mail clerk to accounting clerk on 1 July; Tony Jenkins was promoted from trainee to programmer on 1 March.
Choose a suitable title and arrange the information in any logical order.

Pearson Education Limited
Edinburgh Gate, Harlow
Essex CM20 2JE
England

and Associated Companies throughout the World

First published in Great Britain 1986 by Pitman Publishing
Reprinted with amendments 1989
Reprinted 1990, 1993, 1994
Reprinted by Addison Wesley Longman Limited 1996
Seventh impression 1997
Eigth impression 1998
Ninth impression 1999
Tenth impression 2000

ISBN 0 582 38158 4

British Library Cataloguing-in-Publication Data
A catalogue record for this book is
available from the British Library.

Library of Congress Cataloging-in-Publication Data
A catalog entry for this title is
available from the Library of Congress.

Produced by Pearson Education Asia Pte Ltd
Printed in Singapore (B&JO)

Yr ref JC/TRL special Delivery Accounts Division Kirk & Sons High Street Latham Cornwall CN6 2LG RETURNED CHEQUE Enclosed is our cheque for £612.50 to replace the previous one returned to us. / We are very sorry for any inconvenience we may have caused through our change of bank. We expect to be able to provide a more complete service from now on because our customers will be able to settle our statements through their local banks by a simple transfer of funds. We appreciate yr courteous handling of this matter. / Yrs ffly, Dale Foley, accountant, cc Midland Bank.

Prepare a bulletin board notice for a flatmate. Try to use wording that will screen the unsuitable and incompatible and will attract the like minded.

Prepare a table showing the name, position and starting dates for the following employees of Universal Books: Nancy Powell, cashier, ~~the~~ 1 November 1980; Josh Leeshum, shipper, 16 June 1982; Larry Haliber, receptionist, 1 February 1953; Susan Enright, secretary, 1 September 1979. Arrange in alphabetical order by surname. Title it EMPLOYEE SERVICE. Centre the table horizontally and vertically.

Contents

6

Argus Art Supplies, 315 Tottenham Court Road, London W1, Attention Accounting Dept INVOICE NO 61662 The above invoice for 15 drawing tables has been sent to us in error and we are returning it to you enclosed herewith./ We have received several other invoices from you in the past for goods we did not order. Perhaps we are being confused w The Universal School in Oxford./ Shd any goods be sent in error, we wl ship them back to you at yr expense. Ffy Dale Foley, Accountant

7

You are employed by Donald Hart, a dentist, whose office surgery is at 34 James Street, London W2.

Confirmations of appointments are sent out on post cards one week in advance. Prepare a confirmation of date and time for the 9 am appointment.

THURSDAY 12 JANUARY	
8 AM:	Bill Peters
	17 West Terrace
	W1
9 AM:	Paul King
	231 Chalmers St
	W11
10 AM:	Ken Adams
	97 Draycott Gdns
	NW3

8

You plan to have a holiday and would like a companion. Prepare a notice for the bulletin board describing where you would like to go, how long you will be away, mode of travel, probable cost and the kind of person you are looking for. Be discriminating but flexible.

Preface

This book covers the basic skills of typewriting. It is concise and easy to understand. It explains each aspect of typing thoroughly but in small segments which are easy to learn. Follow the instructions and practise diligently – in return, you will gain the most useful of career skills. This skill will increase with practice and will qualify you for many types of occupation, including high technology occupations.

The *principles* of effective display and of business applications are the same whether you are using a manual, electric or electronic typewriter or a word processor or computer. Whichever machine you use, either now or in the future, you will need to understand and appreciate the different ways in which both general and business matter can be displayed. Although the method of achieving the end result will vary according to the facilities available on your machine, the principles will always stay the same.

These principles of display can be applied in any situation where keyboard skills are used and the section on business applications provides an introduction to the work of a typist. This course, therefore, provides a foundation which can either be used immediately or built upon in the future.

3

Target *stet*
5 minutes

To All Residents

From ~~Resident~~ Manager

REGULATIONS

Several complaints have been received and we would
request that the following regulations be observed.

1 Dust mops are not to be shaken out of the windows

not   2 Guard dogs are/to roam the halls.

3 The reception area is not be used for meetings.

Your cooperation will be appreciated.

4

Target
10 minutes

Don Charles 54 Roads End, Burton, Herts HE8 9RT
Thank you for your manuscript which we have read and found of interest.
Unfortunately, our budget does not permit us to publish it at the moment./Your
approach, though, is a novel one and I am sure that another publishing house
will be interested in talking to you./I am enclosing a list of publishers whose
catalogues are similar to ours and I would suggest you contact some of them./
I wish you success and am truly sorry that we are unable to do anything
further.
Sincerely George Bell Children's Editor

5

Target
15 minutes

SOFTWARE IN INDUSTRY CONFERENCE

list in alphabetical order

Company	Head Office	Representative
Danforth Ltd	Leeds	J L Powers
~~Compute~~ Carr's	Bristol	T C Campbell
~~Robin Hood~~ Regency	Bath	R K Gunderson
Ainsworth & Sons	Sheffield	M R Cowell

Parts of your machine

Manual typewriter

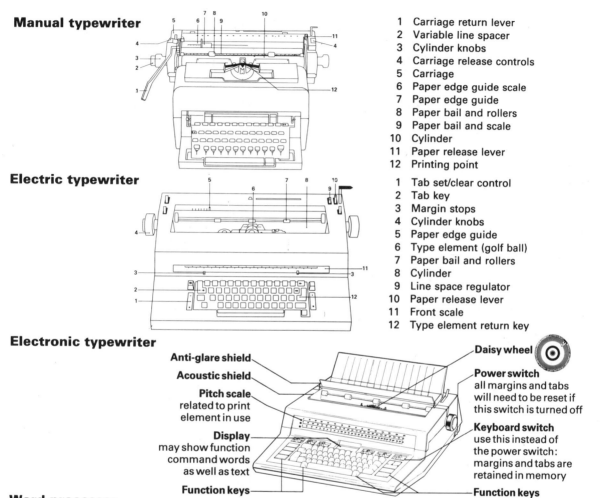

1 Carriage return lever
2 Variable line spacer
3 Cylinder knobs
4 Carriage release controls
5 Carriage
6 Paper edge guide scale
7 Paper edge guide
8 Paper bail and rollers
9 Paper bail and scale
10 Cylinder
11 Paper release lever
12 Printing point

Electric typewriter

1 Tab set/clear control
2 Tab key
3 Margin stops
4 Cylinder knobs
5 Paper edge guide
6 Type element (golf ball)
7 Paper bail and rollers
8 Cylinder
9 Line space regulator
10 Paper release lever
11 Front scale
12 Type element return key

Electronic typewriter

Anti-glare shield

Acoustic shield

Pitch scale
related to print
element in use

Display
may show function
command words
as well as text

Function keys

Daisy wheel

Power switch
all margins and tabs
will need to be reset if
this switch is turned off

Keyboard switch
use this instead of
the power switch:
margins and tabs are
retained in memory

Function keys

Word processor

This can be a computer with a word processing program or a computer used for word processing only (a dedicated word processor). Special commands are used (through function keys or keyboard codes) to manipulate the text.

Visual display
unit (VDU) –
also called
monitor or screen

Numeric
keypad

Function keys

Function keys

1

End of course tests

The following tasks will enable you to judge your progress. Each one requires more than simple copying. You will have to plan your work and decide how to display your work attractively.

Make corrections as needed and be sure to proofread carefully before you remove the paper from the machine.

Follow any instructions that are given. If there are none, use your judgement. If you are not satisfied with your work, repeat the task.

None of the tasks is beyond your ability but do take care to do them correctly. Time yourself and try to stay within the target time.

1

Target
10 minutes

BARBECUE & DISCO ← spaced capitals
Saturday 15 February
       SOUTH ROAD HALL   3 lines of clear space
       6pm for 6.30pm
       Tickets at the door
              £4
    Drinks will be on sale.
Disco to follow 8pm till midnight

2

Target
15 minutes

Itinerary for Mr Barnes

Date	City	Hotel
11 September	Oxford	Three Trees Inn
14 September	Nottingham	King Edward Hotel
16 September	Darlington	Crown Hotel
18 September	Birmingham	Wainwright Hotel
12	Cambridge	Albany Hotel

Section 1 Keyboard mastery

Posture; fingers; home row

Posture

Good posture keeps the typist relaxed in mind and body and is a major factor in developing typing skill.

Poor posture results in fatigue and inefficiency so it is important that you form good habits, paying attention to each detail.

Fingers

Your fingers should be curved, quite tightly for a manual and less so for an electric. Your wrists must be flat.

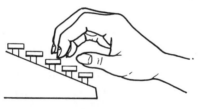

Notice that the steep slope of a manual machine requires a tight curve to the fingers.

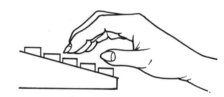

The flatter keyboard on an electric machine or computer requires less curve to the fingers.

Home row

Place your index fingers *very lightly* on **F** and **J**, then spread the other fingers, one to a key, on the same row. Your left hand will cover **A S D F** and your right hand, **J K L ;**. These keys are called the *home row*.

Check!

Use this checklist to be sure that your posture is correct:

* Feet – flat on the floor
* Back – straight but relaxed
* Shoulders – forward and relaxed
* Elbows – close to your ribs
* Forearms – parallel to slope of keyboard
* Wrists – flat
* Fingers – curved

Sit like this

Compose It Yourself

Prepare and type a memo from Alice White to Peter Barnes dated 17 April, telling him that anyone taking holidays in June or September will get an extra week of paid holidays at Christmas time. Ask him to inform his staff and circulate the list again.

Prepare a reply from Peter Barnes dated 19 April asking if the extra week can be taken before Christmas or after the New Year. At least half of the department are interested, which could leave us short staffed at the year end. Are there any other times the extra week could be taken?

Answer from Alice White 20 April that no more than 2 staff should be away at the same time so the extra week can be taken any time between 1 Nov and 28 Feb.

Type the following memos.

Apply Your Skill

TASK 1

To Personnel Dept   PJL/yoi
From Jessie Longhurst   31 May 1986

RESIGNATION NORAH BROWNLEE - 15 August

Please post this vacancy for staff as experience in any department would be useful. Norah is presently earning £9500 as my unofficial PA but someone coming in should start no higher than £8500 and probably closer to £7500. The job requires typing speed of 50 and good English and maths. I'd prefer someone 25 or older.

TASK 2

To All Staff   NER/yoi

From Personnel Director   5 June 1986

POSITION AVAILABLE - Clerk Typist - Accounts - 15 July

In keeping with company policy we hope to promote from within. Only if we are unable to do so will outside applicants be considered.

Preparing to key

Stroking action

Every key stroke, even the very first one you ever make, is fast. Strike every key as if it were red hot and release it instantly. Use an inward pulling motion just as if your fingers were 'running on the spot'. Keep the hands, elbows and shoulders as quiet as possible.

Increasing speed

As you practise, using the correct fingering, the long pauses between strokes will get shorter because your fingers will remember the stroking patterns you have learned. Since every stroke is fast, the only way typing speed increases is by shortening the pauses between strokes. For this reason, you should relax as you type and let your skill grow from day to day.

Paper insertion

You will notice a numbering scale on the metal strip that lies against the roller (cylinder) of your machine. Set the paper guide, the adjustable metal piece behind the cylinder, at 0 so the left-hand edge of your paper will be at 0.

Open the paper release (a lever on the top of the machine, usually on the right) to adjust the paper if necessary and also to remove the paper.

Type sizes

There are 2 sizes of type available, elite (12 characters to the inch) and pica (10 characters to the inch). The size of type determines how many characters you can type across the page.

`This is pica type. This is elite type.`

Modern electric typewriters adjust the spacing between the letters so that characters are spaced 10 to the inch (10 pitch), 12 to the inch (12 pitch) and 15 to the inch (15 pitch).

`This is 10 pitch.    This is 12 pitch.    This is 15 pitch.`

Type styles

By changing the element (golf ball) or daisy wheel on a modern electric or electronic machine, the typist can choose from a variety of typefaces. This provides for versatility not previously possible.

Margins

Find the margin setting controls on your machine. There will be 2 controls, one for the left margin and one for the right. In general, set margins of at least one inch on each side of the paper.

TASK 3   Type the following form triple spaced, remove the paper from the machine then reinsert it. Type your own details in the spaces.

Name _____

Address _____

Telephone _____

Date of Birth ....

Place of Birth ....

Marital Status ....

Printed memo forms

Printed memo forms are in common use. Many firms use a standard form with prepacked carbons. These forms can be purchased readily and cheaply because there is no need for a printed letterhead on interoffice correspondence.

MEMORANDUM

From .... Dan Lewis ....   *Ref* .... DL/YOI ....

To .... All Staff ....   *Date* .... 15 December 198- ....

CHRISTMAS HOLIDAY

This office will close at noon on 24 December and will open on 29 December.

Best wishes to all for a happy Christmas.

DL

Line spacing

The line space regulator is a lever on the top of the machine. It shows 3 settings, usually single, double and triple. Some machines use single, 1½ and double. Double spaced work is typed on every second line, triple spaced on every third.

```
Line 1  This        This        This        This
     2  is                      is
                     is
     3  single                  is
     4  spacing      1½                      is
     5                           double
                     spacing
     6
     7                           spacing     triple
```

Returning the carriage

At the end of the line, you must return the carriage to go on the next line. If you are using an electric or an electronic typewriter, reach with the little finger of your right hand and tap the return key; the other fingers should not move. With a manual, use your left hand, which moves sideways, palm down. Hit the carriage return lever so the index finger strikes the lever between the first and second knuckles. Do not grasp the lever; pretend that it is red hot, too, and return the left hand to the home row immediately.

Space bar

The space bar is a long bar at the bottom of the keyboard. It is controlled with either thumb, using an inward motion. Always use the same thumb.

Beginning to type

Check your posture and place your fingers lightly on the home row. Watch your hands as you type **FJFJFJFJ** till you are satisfied with your stroking. Your hands should be motionless; all the action is in your fingers.

Type several lines, watching your hands and keeping them as quiet as possible. If using a manual machine stroke evenly; with an electric you need only the lightest touch. With either, keep your hands close to the keyboard but *do not rest your hands on the frame of the machine.* Try to relax as you type. Do not worry about errors now. Use correct techniques and keyboard control will grow. Set left margin at 10 pica or 12 elite. For now, you will not require a right margin.

Typing the home row

First fingers	fj	fj	fj	fj	fj	fj	fj	fj	fj	fj	fj	fj
Second fingers	dk	dk	dk	dk	dk	dk	dk	dk	dk	dk	dk	dk
Third fingers	sl	sl	sl	sl	sl	sl	sl	sl	sl	sl	sl	sl
Little fingers	a;	a;	a;	a;	a;	a;	a;	a;	a;	a;	a;	a;

Paper alignment; printed forms

Exact alignment of paper

The paper is held against the cylinder by rollers on the paper bail and by a card holder, often clear plastic.

The lines on the card holder are used for aligning the paper or realigning it if it has been removed and must be reinserted.

The vertical lines will bear a relationship to the centred letters such as I and i. Machines differ one from the other in their alignment so it is necessary to note this relationship before the paper is removed in order to realign it exactly.

The horizontal lines relate to the bottoms of the letters that have no descenders (parts of the letters which descend below the line such as in g, p and y). Note whether the line of type sits on the line, is above or below, and if so, by how much.

Type this line:

```
Poor John never learned to type.
```

Examine closely the relationship of lines on the card holders to the line of type.

Remove the paper from the machine then reinsert it, re-establishing the relationship by using the paper release to adjust the paper so that it is straight, and the variable line spacer for vertical adjustment.

Retype the same line directly on top.

If you have realigned exactly the type will appear emboldened. If it is not exactly aligned, decide how it can be improved then try again.

Printed forms for completion

Many office tasks involve the completion of printed forms that may be carefully designed to conform to the line spacing of the typewriter.

When typing on lines, solid or dotted, align the paper so the line of type, including descenders, completely clears the line.

Notice how legible the typing is when the line of type is slightly above the line.

```
foggy day      foggy day
```

TASK 1

Using the underscore, type a solid line across the page. Remove the paper then reinsert it. Type 'happy' several times, using the ratchet release or the left cylinder knob pushed in, to experiment with the alignment.

TASK 2

Type a dotted line using closed dots and repeat the exercise, typing 'happy' several times. You will notice that the dots strike the paper a little higher than the underscore so allow for that.

Punctuation; the home keys

Punctuation

Punctuation becomes part of the word it follows. Space after punctuation but not before. The semi colon is followed by 1 space.

CHECK!

Check your posture before you begin to type the lines below. If you forget where a letter is, look at the chart but try not to look at your hands. *Do not* look up at the end of a line; return the carriage and go on to the next line.

Use A4 paper. Type each line 3 times. Set left margin at 10 pica or 12 elite.

Drill

```
1 fj fj dk dk sl sl a; a; asdf ;lkj as as
2 fj fj dk dk sl sl a; a; asdf ;lkj ff jj
3 dd kk ss ll aa ;; as as ask ask all all
```

Words

```
4 lad lad dad dad sad sad fad fad add add
5 all all add add ask ask lad lad fad fad
```

Phrases

```
6 a sad fall; a dad adds; ask a sad lass;
7 all fall; all sad; all sad salads fall;
```

Speed

```
8 a lad falls; ask a lad; dad adds salad;

....1....2....3....4....5....6....7....8
```

Measuring your speed

Typing speed is measured in words per minute, based on 5 characters to a word. Each letter, space and punctuation mark is a character. There is a word count at the end of each drill so you can closely monitor your progress from day to day.

Type each line for one minute. If you finish the line, repeat it until the minute is up. Count the number of words you have typed using the word count line below the line of typing. Keep a record of your speed for each day. If you make more than 2 errors in the minute you should practise the words with errors and then try the speed test again.

Memos

A memo (memorandum) is a message sent from one department or person to another within the company.

Memos are often typed on printed forms but can be typed on plain paper using a format similar to the one below. It is usually brief and to the point and nearly always has a subject line.

In general, leave 1 inch margins and begin typing 1 inch from the top of the page.

TASK 1

Type the following memo on A5 landscape. Leave 2 spaces after the longest lines in the heading on each side (From: and Date:). Line up the line above or below.

Use single spacing except above the subject heading. Leave 2 clear line spaces there to separate the top and bottom of the memo.

```
MEMORANDUM

From:   Alice White          Ref:    AW/yoi

To:     Peter Barnes         Date:   15 April 1986


SUMMER HOLIDAYS

Please circulate a list through your section, asking for
holiday preferences.  We will do our best to accommodate the
choices.

Since we are bringing in special relief staff to cover the
period 15 June to 30 September, please be sure that all
holidays are taken in that time.
```

TASK 2

Using the same format, type an answer from Peter Barnes to Alice White dated the following day.

```
SUMMER HOLIDAYS

I have circulated the holiday list and the requests are
very heavy for July and August but very light for June
and September.

How many people can be away at the same time?
```

Letters E and H

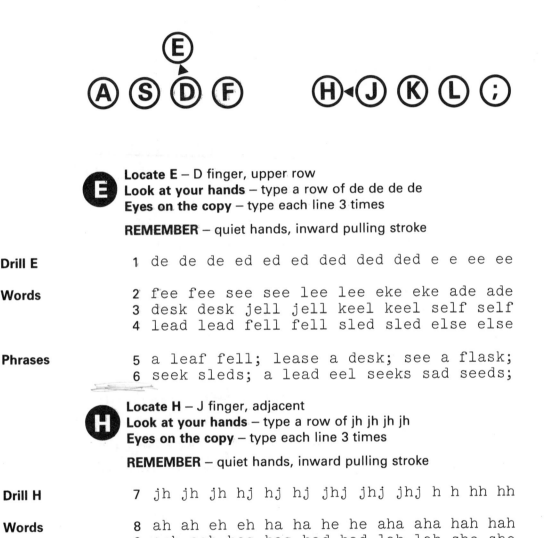

Locate E – D finger, upper row
Look at your hands – type a row of de de de de
Eyes on the copy – type each line 3 times

REMEMBER – quiet hands, inward pulling stroke

Drill E

1 de de de ed ed ed ded ded ded e e ee ee

Words

2 fee fee see see lee lee eke eke ade ade
3 desk desk jell jell keel keel self self
4 lead lead fell fell sled sled else else

Phrases

5 a leaf fell; lease a desk; see a flask;
6 seek sleds; a lead eel seeks sad seeds;

Locate H – J finger, adjacent
Look at your hands – type a row of jh jh jh jh
Eyes on the copy – type each line 3 times

REMEMBER – quiet hands, inward pulling stroke

Drill H

7 jh jh jh hj hj hj jhj jhj jhj h h hh hh

Words

8 ah ah eh eh ha ha he he aha aha hah hah
9 ash ash has has had had lah lah she she
10 shah shah shad shad hall hall half half

Phrases

11 a shelf held a shell; she added a sled;
12 a flea shed a leaf; he had half a shed;

Speed

13 sell a seal a flea; sell a flea a lake;
14 a leaf shades a shed; he shakes a leaf;

....1....2....3....4....5....6....7....8

6

Type the following letters with a carbon copy and envelope for each. Take care to space them attractively. Karen Stanhope will sign them. Use the current date.

a   *Your ref TGC:kmv, Clover Industries, 554 Randall Road, Tippington, Sussex, WE8 9YG, Attention Thomas Granger, Dear Sirs NEW TITLES Thank you for the interest you have shown in our catalogue featuring new titles for the autumn./We are enclosing the midseason supplement which should bring you up to date with our complete line./Please contact me directly for any more information you would like. Yours faithfully, UNIVERSAL BOOKS, Sales Division, enc.*

b   SPECIAL DELIVERY Leonard Carlson 56 Pine Grove Linden Wilts WT6 3NL Dear Sir
Royalty Cheque We are enclosing a cheque for £2000 to cover the first quarter as per your royalty statement./ Yours sincerely enc cc Accounting

c   Wise Owl Books, 9 High Street Pembird Middx MD6 2RL Attention Mrs Lily Tennes Dear Sirs In reply to your request I have spoken to our public relations executive and she will be very happy to arrange to send a representative to your book fair./ We will be pleased to receive all the details./ Yrs. ffy.

Letter O; Review

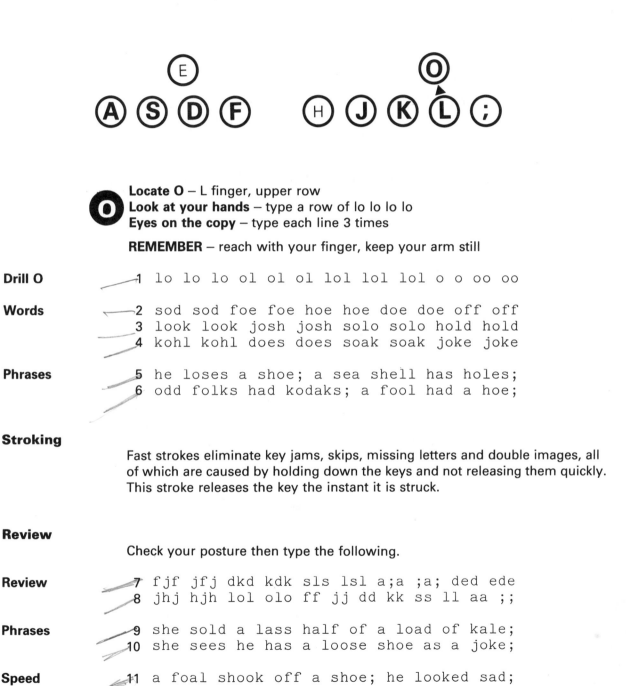

Locate O – L finger, upper row
Look at your hands – type a row of lo lo lo lo
Eyes on the copy – type each line 3 times

REMEMBER – reach with your finger, keep your arm still

Drill O

1 lo lo lo ol ol ol lol lol lol o o oo oo

Words

2 sod sod foe foe hoe hoe doe doe off off
3 look look josh josh solo solo hold hold
4 kohl kohl does does soak soak joke joke

Phrases

5 he loses a shoe; a sea shell has holes;
6 odd folks had kodaks; a fool had a hoe;

Stroking

Fast strokes eliminate key jams, skips, missing letters and double images, all of which are caused by holding down the keys and not releasing them quickly. This stroke releases the key the instant it is struck.

Review

Check your posture then type the following.

Review

7 fjf jfj dkd kdk sls lsl a;a ;a; ded ede
8 jhj hjh lol olo ff jj dd kk ss ll aa ;;

Phrases

9 she sold a lass half of a load of kale;
10 she sees he has a loose shoe as a joke;

Speed

11 a foal shook off a shoe; he looked sad;

....1....2....3....4....5....6....7....8

7

Attention line

Use the attention line to direct the letter to the person who will deal with it.

The house style of your employer will determine which form to use, but it is quickest to type it in capitals.

Use a group salutation with an attention line:

Dear Sirs   Letter to company, department, section, division, corporation, any group of males, males and females or a group whose composition is not known.

Ladies   YWCA, Women's Institute, any all female group.

TASK

Prepare the following for signature, ie type the letter on A5, take a carbon copy, and type the envelope.

KS/yoi

11 December 1986

Southern School Supplies Ltd
223 Kensworth Road
LONDON SE9

ATTENTION: PURCHASING AGENT

Dear Sirs

In reply to your telephone enquiry, we have a full range of notebooks and stationery supplies in addition to texts and trade books.

If you would be interested in visiting our showrooms, please telephone me and I shall make arrangements for you to view our complete lines.

We appreciate your interest in UNIVERSAL BOOKS, and I hope to hear from you soon.

Yours sincerely

Karen Stanhope
Sales Division

Letters R and U

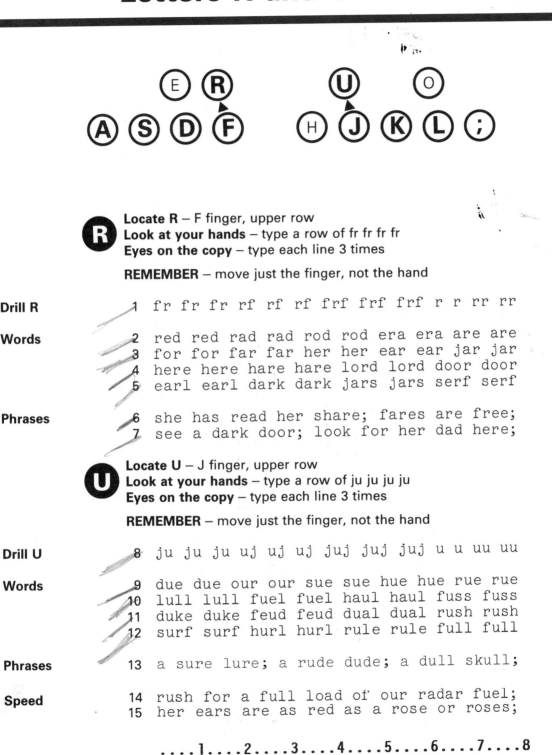

R Locate R – F finger, upper row
Look at your hands – type a row of fr fr fr fr
Eyes on the copy – type each line 3 times

REMEMBER – move just the finger, not the hand

Drill R   1   fr fr fr rf rf rf frf frf frf r r rr rr

Words   2   red red rad rad rod rod era era are are
          3   for for far far her her ear ear jar jar
          4   here here hare hare lord lord door door
          5   earl earl dark dark jars jars serf serf

Phrases   6   she has read her share; fares are free;
            7   see a dark door; look for her dad here;

U Locate U – J finger, upper row
Look at your hands – type a row of ju ju ju ju
Eyes on the copy – type each line 3 times

REMEMBER – move just the finger, not the hand

Drill U   8   ju ju ju uj uj uj juj juj juj u u uu uu

Words   9   due due our our sue sue hue hue rue rue
         10   lull lull fuel fuel haul haul fuss fuss
         11   duke duke feud feud dual dual rush rush
         12   surf surf hurl hurl rule rule full full

Phrases   13   a sure lure; a rude dude; a dull skull;

Speed   14   rush for a full load of our radar fuel;
        15   her ears are as red as a rose or roses;

....1....2....3....4....5....6....7....8

8

Enclosures

Enclosures or enc

This is a signal to the mail room or the person opening the envelope that there is something inside besides the letter. If there is more than one enclosure, the notation will read 'encs 4' or whatever the exact number of enclosures is. Marginal marks may be used in addition to or instead of the enclosure notation. Marginal marks are used in the left margin on each line an enclosure is described. Type 3 dots beginning ½ inch to the left of the text.

TASK

Type the following letter on A4. Take a carbon copy, and type the envelope.

```
Our ref NER/yoi
Your ref JS/toi

15 January 1986

CONFIDENTIAL

Miss J Spencer
Western Industries Limited
Davenport Road
LONDON W14

Dear Miss Spencer

ANTHONY JAMES CORNELL

This will confirm that the above named was in our employ from
1 October 1976 to 30 June 1984 as mail room supervisor. His
position description is enclosed.

We found him to be a conscientious and diligent worker and we
were sorry to lose him when he accepted a position with more
opportunities for advancement.

Yours faithfully


N E Ramsay
Personnel Director

enc
```

Shift keys

The shift keys

Each key on the typewriter will produce 2 characters called upper and lower case. Only lower case characters — small letters — have been used so far.

Capitals are upper case. To type an upper case character, press a shift key at the same time the letter key is struck.

In order to type a perfect capital, the shift key must be fully depressed at the instant the key strikes the paper. Use a count of 3 — shift, strike, release shift.

To type a capital of any letter controlled by the left hand, use the right shift key. For a capital of any letter using the right hand, use the left shift key. Shift with one hand, strike with the other.

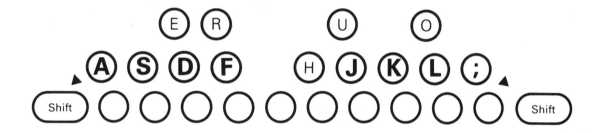

Left shift

Locate left shift — A finger, lower corner
Look at your hands — shift, strike J, release shift
Type: J J H H K K L L O O U U
Lola Jud Karl Olaf Harold

REMEMBER — try to move only the A finger to shift; try not to move the S, D and F fingers

Right shift

Locate right shift — ; finger, lower corner
Look at your hands — shift, strike F, release shift
Type: F F D D S S A A E E R R
Fred Dee Sue Ada Ella Rose

REMEMBER — try to move only the ; finger to shift; try not to move the L, K and J fingers

Subject line; carbon copy – cc

Subject line

This tells, in a few words, the subject of the letter in order that it may be easily located in the file. The subject line is also helpful in directing a letter that has no attention line (see page 82).

The subject line may be typed in several ways but it is quickest to type it in capitals eg SUMMER HOLIDAYS.

Carbon copy cc

This notation, designated cc, shows the names of those people who have been sent a carbon copy of the letter. It would also show departments or companies.

TASK

Type the following letter on A5. Take 2 carbon copies, type the envelope and fold the letter for insertion into the envelope.

```
AC/yoi

12 October 1986

Mr Stanley Collins
Collins Printing
99 Vander Road
KIPLEY
Kent  K15 8JL

Dear Mr Collins

QUOTATION - BUSINESS AS USUAL

Further to our recent telephone conversation, would you
please send us written confirmation of your quotation.

We are prepared to contract your company to print our
new book, BUSINESS AS USUAL, and require confirmation
promptly in order to assess our costs.

Yours faithfully


Andrew Cabeldu
Production Director

cc P Jessica Langhurst, Controller
```

. ; stroking; review

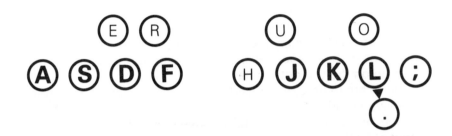

Locate. – L finger, lower row
Look at your hands – type a row of l. l. l. l.
Eyes on the copy – type each line 3 times

REMEMBER – the other fingers will rise as you reach to the lower row. A full stop after a sentence is followed by 2 spaces

Sentences

1 Sue heard a fall. She also heard larks.
2 Lou has a fear of Al. Al fears Joe Lee.
3 Leo read for Karl. Fred asked for Ella.
4 Hal looked for Des. Des fell for Laura.

Stroking

Avoid clinging to or clutching the home row keys. They serve best as anchors (especially **A** and ;) during the early stages of learning to type. Resting the fingers on them will hamper your skill development.

Review

Check your posture then type the following.

Words

5 of of or or us us so so do do he he a a
6 her her our our ear ear led led fee fee
7 see see sod sod oar oar sue sue has has
8 she she are are had had for for ask ask

Sentences

9 He has a dark horse. He has all falls.
10 Rush hours are dull. Share rush hours.

Speed

11 All of us offered a rose for her dress.
12 Rose asked for a leaf salad for a flea.

....1....2....3....4....5....6....7....8

Taking carbon copies

Carbon copies

A copy of every letter is kept in the file. It may be photocopied or the typist can make a carbon copy.

To take a carbon copy place the flimsy paper for the carbon copy on the desk, place the carbon paper shiny side down on top of it, place the letterhead right side up on the top of the pile.

Take care to assemble this correctly or the copy of the letter will appear on the reverse side of the letterhead.

Handle carbon paper carefully to avoid wrinkling it and causing marks to appear on the carbon copies.

TASK

Type this letter on A5. Take a carbon copy, type the envelope and fold the letter.

NER/yoi

22 November 1986

Miss Eleanor Caine
17 North Gardens
LONDON E3

Dear Miss Caine

We are pleased to offer you employment as a clerk-typist beginning 1 December at a salary of £6,000 per annum, rising to £7,800. Additional training will be available to you at our expense and will open the door for promotion within the company.

Upon receipt of this letter, would you please confirm by letter or telephone in order that we may prepare the necessary documents.

Welcome to Universal Books, Miss Caine.

Yours sincerely
UNIVERSAL BOOKS

N E Ramsay
Personnel Director

Letters I and N

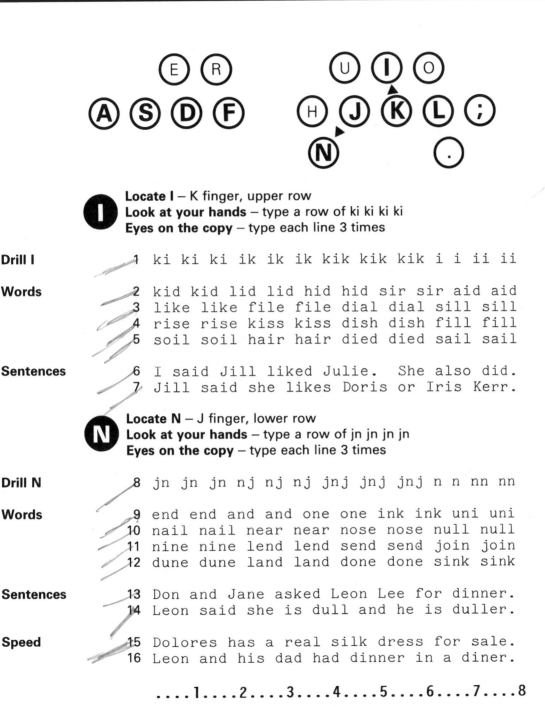

I
Locate I – K finger, upper row
Look at your hands – type a row of ki ki ki ki
Eyes on the copy – type each line 3 times

Drill I
1 ki ki ki ik ik ik kik kik kik i i ii ii

Words
2 kid kid lid lid hid hid sir sir aid aid
3 like like file file dial dial sill sill
4 rise rise kiss kiss dish dish fill fill
5 soil soil hair hair died died sail sail

Sentences
6 I said Jill liked Julie. She also did.
7 Jill said she likes Doris or Iris Kerr.

N
Locate N – J finger, lower row
Look at your hands – type a row of jn jn jn jn
Eyes on the copy – type each line 3 times

Drill N
8 jn jn jn nj nj nj jnj jnj jnj n n nn nn

Words
9 end end and and one one ink ink uni uni
10 nail nail near near nose nose null null
11 nine nine lend lend send send join join
12 dune dune land land done done sink sink

Sentences
13 Don and Jane asked Leon Lee for dinner.
14 Leon said she is dull and he is duller.

Speed
15 Dolores has a real silk dress for sale.
16 Leon and his dad had dinner in a diner.

....1....2....3....4....5....6....7....8

Envelopes; folding letters

Envelopes

Envelopes are addressed like post cards. Begin typing approximately half the way down and roughly centre the longest line.

Most business letters are posted in size C5/6 envelopes, which measure approximately 4¼ in x 8⅝ in.

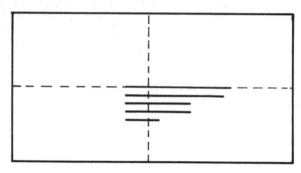

TASK

Cut paper to represent envelopes and address one to each of the following.

a Miss Eleanor Collins
  27 Denton Row
  WATFORD
  Herts   WD4 7AP

b CONFIDENTIAL

  Mr Ivan Campbell
  Manager, Bookmasters
  15 Kings Row
  SOUTHAMPTON
  SO3 9HT

c SPECIAL DELIVERY

  Mr Tom Borden
  334 Eastern Road
  SHEFFIELD
  S7 3EG

Folding letters

A letter on A4 is folded into 3 and on A5 is folded into 2, when being placed in C5/6 envelopes.

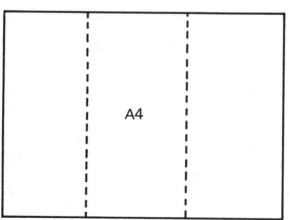

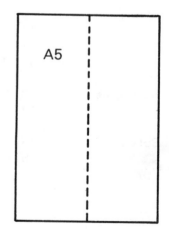

Letter T; review

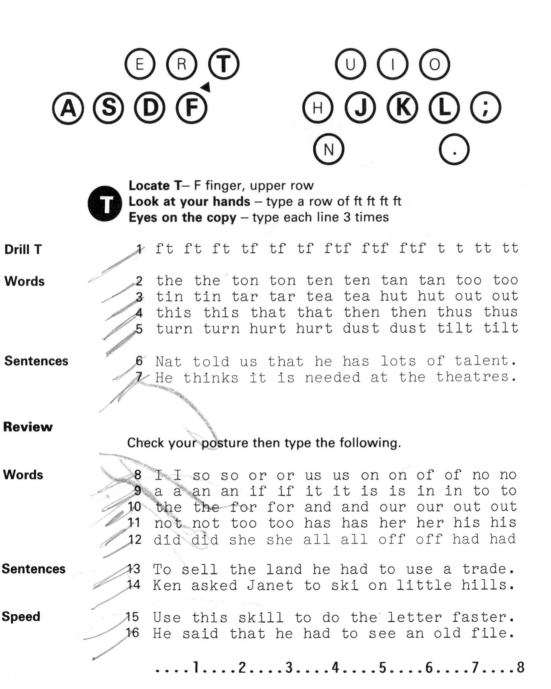

Locate T – F finger, upper row
Look at your hands – type a row of ft ft ft ft
Eyes on the copy – type each line 3 times

Drill T

```
1  ft ft ft tf tf tf ftf ftf ftf t t tt tt
```

Words

```
2  the the ton ton ten ten tan tan too too
3  tin tin tar tar tea tea hut hut out out
4  this this that that then then thus thus
5  turn turn hurt hurt dust dust tilt tilt
```

Sentences

```
6  Nat told us that he has lots of talent.
7  He thinks it is needed at the theatres.
```

Review

Check your posture then type the following.

Words

```
8  I I so so or or us us on on of of no no
9  a a an an if if it it is is in in to to
10 the the for for and and our our out out
11 not not too too has has her her his his
12 did did she she all all off off had had
```

Sentences

```
13 To sell the land he had to use a trade.
14 Ken asked Janet to ski on little hills.
```

Speed

```
15 Use this skill to do the letter faster.
16 He said that he had to see an old file.
```

```
....1....2....3....4....5....6....7....8
```

Other display lines

There are various additional display lines which may need to be included in a letter. These are shown on the next 6 pages. Note there is still one line of space above and below each line.

Your reference

If a letter is a specific reply, quoting the addressee's reference will simplify the procedure when your letter is received.

Special instructions

Special notes such as CONFIDENTIAL or URGENT, and special instructions such as REGISTERED or SPECIAL DELIVERY are typed before the inside address and are copied on the envelope as part of the address. It is quicker to type this in capitals. Type the following letter on A4 paper.

TASK
```
Your ref KLG:nh
Our ref PJL:wsa

15 September 1986

REGISTERED

Mr Keith Gordon
52 Perry Lane
BRENTFORD
Middx  BT3 8YT

Dear Mr Gordon

This will confirm our acceptance of your bid for cabinet work in
our offices according to our agreed specifications.

Unless we hear from you to the contrary within 72 hours by registered
post, we will assume that you are prepared to begin work on 1 November.

Yours faithfully



P Jessica Langhurst
Controller
```

Letters G and Y

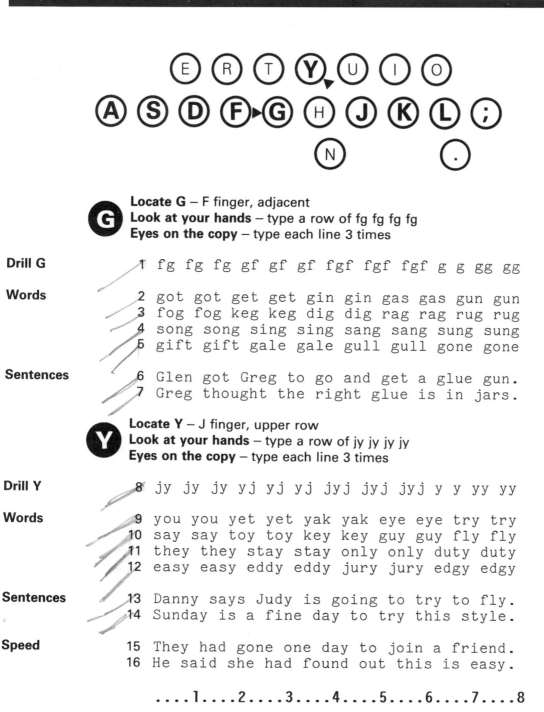

G
Locate G – F finger, adjacent
Look at your hands – type a row of fg fg fg fg
Eyes on the copy – type each line 3 times

Drill G

1 fg fg fg gf gf gf fgf fgf fgf g g gg gg

Words

2 got got get get gin gin gas gas gun gun
3 fog fog keg keg dig dig rag rag rug rug
4 song song sing sing sang sang sung sung
5 gift gift gale gale gull gull gone gone

Sentences

6 Glen got Greg to go and get a glue gun.
7 Greg thought the right glue is in jars.

Y
Locate Y – J finger, upper row
Look at your hands – type a row of jy jy jy jy
Eyes on the copy – type each line 3 times

Drill Y

8 jy jy jy yj yj yj jyj jyj jyj y y yy yy

Words

9 you you yet yet yak yak eye eye try try
10 say say toy toy key key guy guy fly fly
11 they they stay stay only only duty duty
12 easy easy eddy eddy jury jury edgy edgy

Sentences

13 Danny says Judy is going to try to fly.
14 Sunday is a fine day to try this style.

Speed

15 They had gone one day to join a friend.
16 He said she had found out this is easy.

....1....2....3....4....5....6....7....8

Complimentary closes

Signature block — in-house style

There are several possible lines that may be added to the complimentary close. These are optional and vary from company to company. Any or all may be used.

Type each of these closings.

1
Yours faithfully

David Graham

2
Yours faithfully

David Graham
Training Consultant

3
Yours faithfully
UNIVERSAL BOOKS

4
Yours faithfully
UNIVERSAL BOOKS

David Graham

5
Yours faithfully
UNIVERSAL BOOKS

David Graham
Training Consultant

Company name

A business letter can be legally binding and it is essential that the typist remember that the letter is sent by the company, not the person signing it.

Name of dictator

This is often included because a typewritten name can always be read. A signature may be illegible or confusing.

Title

This is useful information for the recipient of the letter.

Letter W; review

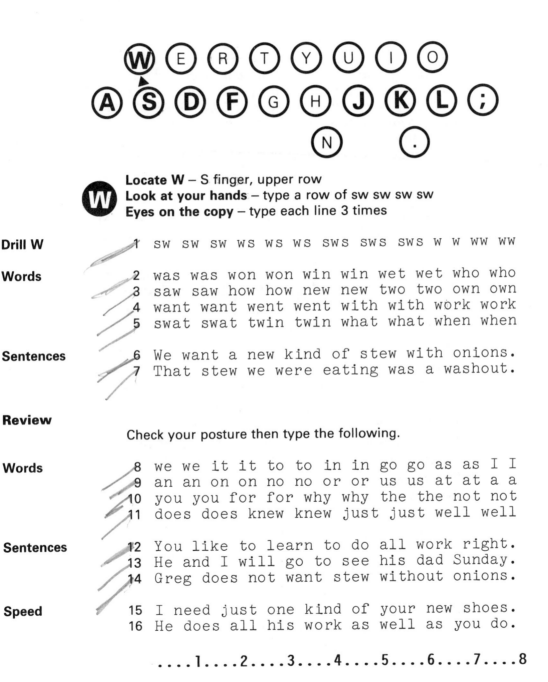

Locate W – S finger, upper row
Look at your hands – type a row of sw sw sw sw
Eyes on the copy – type each line 3 times

Drill W

1 SW SW SW WS WS WS SWS SWS SWS W W WW WW

Words

2 was was won won win win wet wet who who
3 saw saw how how new new two two own own
4 want want went went with with work work
5 swat swat twin twin what what when when

Sentences

6 We want a new kind of stew with onions.
7 That stew we were eating was a washout.

Review

Check your posture then type the following.

Words

8 we we it it to to in in go go as as I I
9 an an on on no no or or us us at at a a
10 you you for for why why the the not not
11 does does knew knew just just well well

Sentences

12 You like to learn to do all work right.
13 He and I will go to see his dad Sunday.
14 Greg does not want stew without onions.

Speed

15 I need just one kind of your new shoes.
16 He does all his work as well as you do.

....1....2....3....4....5....6....7....8

Apply Your Skill

1 Type the letter on page 74.
2 Type the following letters from Elaine Selkirk on A4 paper. Remember you may leave extra space before the reference if the letter is short.

a *Mr Donald Hughes/15 Crescent Gardens/Hawthorne/Kent GT3 5LM/Dear Mr Hughes/Thank you for the interest you have shown in our instructional material for schools and seminars. We are proud, indeed, of what we can offer you./All our books are printed on high quality paper, specially treated to be resistant to tearing. The covers are coated with mylar to keep them new looking and to protect them from water damage./We feature regular in-house training for our customers in order to keep them abreast of new methods, research findings and materials. There is no charge for these./We also provide a special instruction team who can come at your request to demonstrate our products and methods. If you can't come to us, then we will come to you. Once again, no charge./If I can offer any further help, please feel free to contact me./Yours sincerely.*

b

Miss Jocelyn Tate / 231 Gt. Portland St. / London W1 / Dear Miss Tate / I am very sorry that I was out of the office when you were here yesterday. / The brochure you left is of some interest to us. I would be very pleased to discuss it with you and perhaps place an order. / Since this is a very busy season for us, I have a full schedule. I have booked an appointment for you next Friday at 11 am. If that is not convenient for you, please telephone me to make other arrangements. / Would it be possible for you to bring samples when you come? I would be interested in seeing a complete catalogue of your products. / I would also be interested in the options for financing any orders we might place with you. Please bring all the relevant data with you. / I am looking forward to our meeting; your product line is certainly innovative as well as attractive. / Yours sincerely

Letters C and V

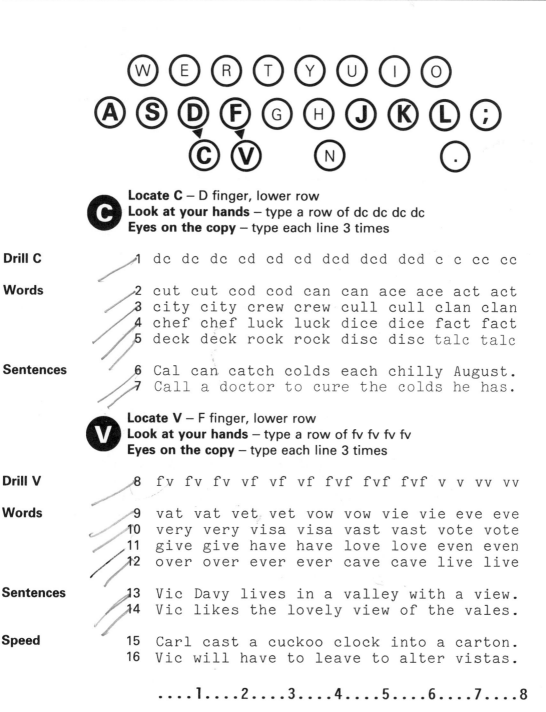

C Locate C – D finger, lower row
Look at your hands – type a row of dc dc dc dc
Eyes on the copy – type each line 3 times

Drill C   1 dc dc dc cd cd cd dcd dcd dcd c c cc cc

Words   2 cut cut cod cod can can ace ace act act
3 city city crew crew cull cull clan clan
4 chef chef luck luck dice dice fact fact
5 deck deck rock rock disc disc talc talc

Sentences   6 Cal can catch colds each chilly August.
7 Call a doctor to cure the colds he has.

V Locate V – F finger, lower row
Look at your hands – type a row of fv fv fv fv
Eyes on the copy – type each line 3 times

Drill V   8 fv fv fv vf vf vf fvf fvf fvf v v vv vv

Words   9 vat vat vet vet vow vow vie vie eve eve
10 very very visa visa vast vast vote vote
11 give give have have love love even even
12 over over ever ever cave cave live live

Sentences   13 Vic Davy lives in a valley with a view.
14 Vic likes the lovely view of the vales.

Speed   15 Carl cast a cuckoo clock into a carton.
16 Vic will have to leave to alter vistas.

....1....2....3....4....5....6....7....8

Business letter A4

Elite 12
Pica 10

DG/yoi
①
27 May 1986
①
Mr J Hanson
15 Montford Place
EWELL
Surrey   CR4 3TW
①
Dear Mr Hanson
①
In response to your inquiry, we are illustrating modern
practice in business correspondence.
①
All letters are single spaced and a line of clear space separates
each section of the letter from the others. A line of clear
space is left between paragraphs.

①   ①
The trend is to clear and concise wording, avoiding 'business   ①"
English' terminology.
①
The complimentary closings vary in formality, yours faithfully
being the most formal and yours sincerely being less so.
①
This letter demonstrates the fully blocked style, in which all
lines begin at the left margin. For this reason, it is fast to
type and, therefore, is popular in many business offices, even
though it may appear somewhat unbalanced. The efficiency more
than makes up for any such drawback.
①
Should there be any further material you require please do not
hesitate to contact me directly, either by letter or by phone.
I am happy to offer my assistance.
①
Yours sincerely

④

David Graham

? and review

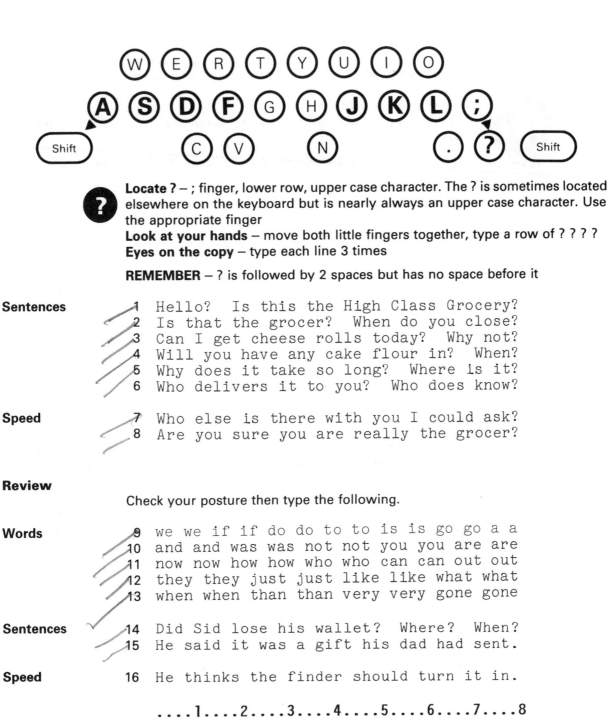

Locate ? – ; finger, lower row, upper case character. The ? is sometimes located elsewhere on the keyboard but is nearly always an upper case character. Use the appropriate finger

Look at your hands – move both little fingers together, type a row of ? ? ? ?

Eyes on the copy – type each line 3 times

REMEMBER – ? is followed by 2 spaces but has no space before it

Sentences

1 Hello? Is this the High Class Grocery?
2 Is that the grocer? When do you close?
3 Can I get cheese rolls today? Why not?
4 Will you have any cake flour in? When?
5 Why does it take so long? Where is it?
6 Who delivers it to you? Who does know?

Speed

7 Who else is there with you I could ask?
8 Are you sure you are really the grocer?

Review

Check your posture then type the following.

Words

9 we we if if do do to to is is go go a a
10 and and was was not not you you are are
11 now now how how who who can can out out
12 they they just just like like what what
13 when when than than very very gone gone

Sentences

14 Did Sid lose his wallet? Where? When?
15 He said it was a gift his dad had sent.

Speed

16 He thinks the finder should turn it in.

....1....2....3....4....5....6....7....8

Body

The trend is to use clear and concise wording. Avoid 'business English' terminology.

Complimentary close

The close varies in formality. Yours faithfully is the most formal, normally used when the letter is not addressed to a person. Yours sincerely is less formal and is normally used when the letter is addressed to a specific person.

1 Type the letter on page 71.
2 Type the following letters dictated by Karen Stanhope. Use the current date.

a *Letter to Joseph Crawford, Purchasing Agent, Hilliard Enterprises, Elston, Lancashire EN4 5LL*

Dear Mr Crawford

In reply to your recent inquiry, BETTER LETTERS will be available within the next 3 months.

We are prepared to offer you a trade discount on orders of 100 or more copies provided we receive your order in the next 2 months. The list price is £3.95 and the terms to you would be 45% discount net 30 days.

If you have any questions about the book please contact me personally.

Yours sincerely

b *Malcolm Dinsmore/Acquisitions Librarian/Austin Branch Library/Morgan/ Kent KY7 9ER/Dear Mr Dinsmore/I plan to be in Morgan on Thursday afternoon, 19 July and would like to arrange a meeting with you regarding our new stock. Would 3 pm be convenient for you?/I shall be bringing you our new catalogue and sample copies of our latest publications as you have requested. Should there be any further materials I can bring, please contact me before 17 July./Yours faithfully*

c *Ellen Sparrow / Manager / The Bookworm / High Street / Hurston / Cornwall CV2 9JL / Dear Miss Sparrow / Further to our telephone conversation this morning, I am sending you (under separate cover) 100 copies of our new spring catalogue. Please contact me if there is anything further you require / Yours sincerely*

Letters M and X

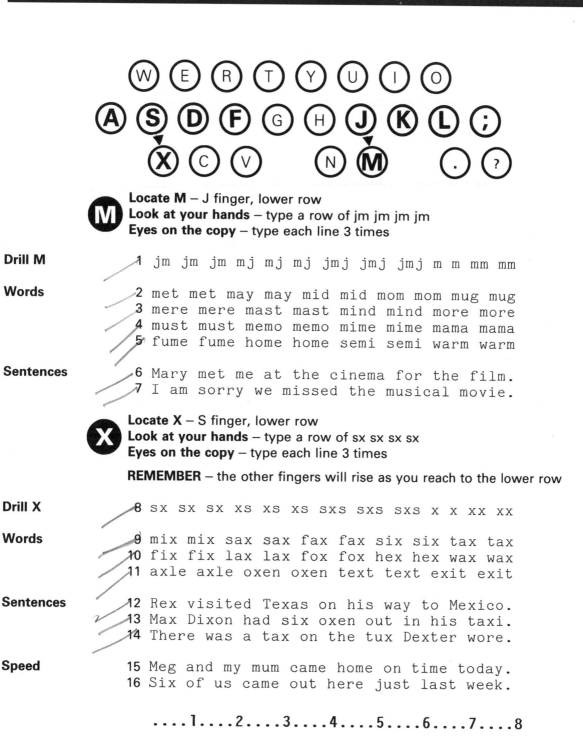

M Locate M – J finger, lower row
Look at your hands – type a row of jm jm jm jm
Eyes on the copy – type each line 3 times

Drill M

1 jm jm jm mj mj mj jmj jmj jmj m m mm mm

Words

2 met met may may mid mid mom mom mug mug
3 mere mere mast mast mind mind more more
4 must must memo memo mime mime mama mama
5 fume fume home home semi semi warm warm

Sentences

6 Mary met me at the cinema for the film.
7 I am sorry we missed the musical movie.

X Locate X – S finger, lower row
Look at your hands – type a row of sx sx sx sx
Eyes on the copy – type each line 3 times

REMEMBER – the other fingers will rise as you reach to the lower row

Drill X

8 sx sx sx xs xs xs sxs sxs sxs x x xx xx

Words

9 mix mix sax sax fax fax six six tax tax
10 fix fix lax lax fox fox hex hex wax wax
11 axle axle oxen oxen text text exit exit

Sentences

12 Rex visited Texas on his way to Mexico.
13 Max Dixon had six oxen out in his taxi.
14 There was a tax on the tux Dexter wore.

Speed

15 Meg and my mum came home on time today.
16 Six of us came out here just last week.

....1....2....3....4....5....6....7....8

Business letters

Since letters are the most common of office tasks, it is important that the typist produces attractive letters quickly and accurately. A letter may be the customer's first or only contact with the company and he/she will judge the company by that letter. Terms and conditions stated in a letter are binding on the company so it is essential that the material be accurate. Business letters can be typed quickly because they follow a similar format.

Letterhead paper

Business letters are typed on letterhead paper.

Spacing

Letters have single spacing and a clear line space separates each new section. A clear line space separates paragraphs. Four lines of space are left for the signature. For short letters, leave additional space before the reference.

Most letters are typed on A4 paper but for reasons of economy, shorter letters are typed on A5 paper. Whenever possible, type a letter on one page.

Open punctuation

Most business letters today use open punctuation; no punctuation is used except in the body of the letter.

Fully blocked style

There are several styles of business letters but the most efficient is the fully blocked style in which all the lines begin at the left margin.

Margins

Margins should not be less than 1 inch for A4 and ¾ inch for A5, and where possible should be equal on each side.

Inside address and envelope

The envelope will be copied directly from the inside address.

Salutation

The salutation, the formal greeting in a letter, is determined by the inside address. Use either the name of the addressee or the less personal form, Dear Sir, for individuals. A group salutation, Dear Sirs or Gentlemen, is used if the letter is addressed to a company.

Letter Q; review

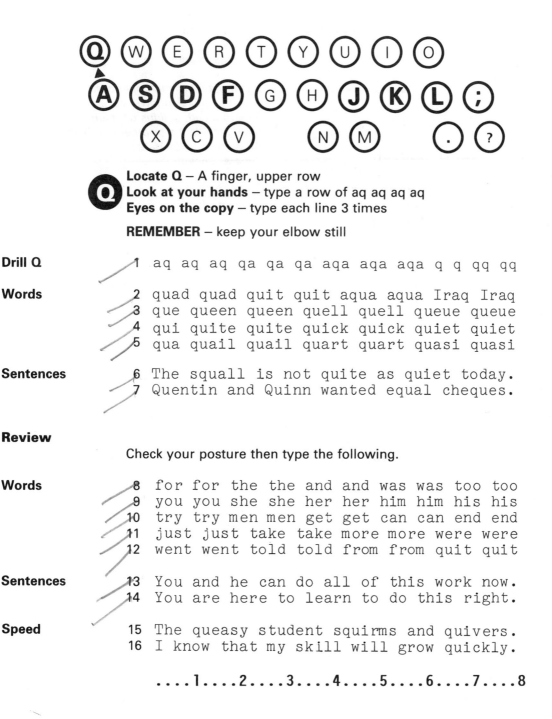

Q Locate Q – A finger, upper row
Look at your hands – type a row of aq aq aq aq
Eyes on the copy – type each line 3 times

REMEMBER – keep your elbow still

Drill Q
1 aq aq aq qa qa qa aqa aqa aqa q q qq qq

Words
2 quad quad quit quit aqua aqua Iraq Iraq
3 que queen queen quell quell queue queue
4 qui quite quite quick quick quiet quiet
5 qua quail quail quart quart quasi quasi

Sentences
6 The squall is not quite as quiet today.
7 Quentin and Quinn wanted equal cheques.

Review

Check your posture then type the following.

Words
8 for for the the and and was was too too
9 you you she she her her him him his his
10 try try men men get get can can end end
11 just just take take more more were were
12 went went told told from from quit quit

Sentences
13 You and he can do all of this work now.
14 You are here to learn to do this right.

Speed
15 The queasy student squirms and quivers.
16 I know that my skill will grow quickly.

....1....2....3....4....5....6....7....8

Business letter A5

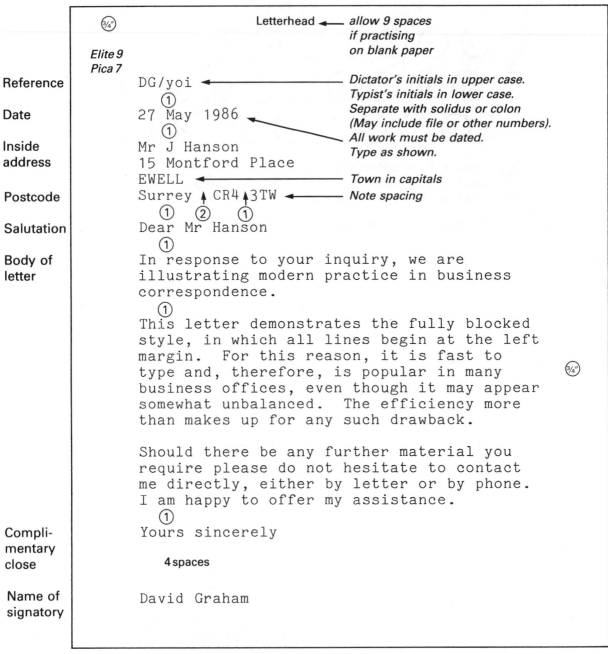

The above is a **fully blocked** letter. Notice that all the lines begin at the left margin and it has open punctuation, except in the body of the letter.
See pages 72-3 for explanations of parts of letters.

Letters P and B

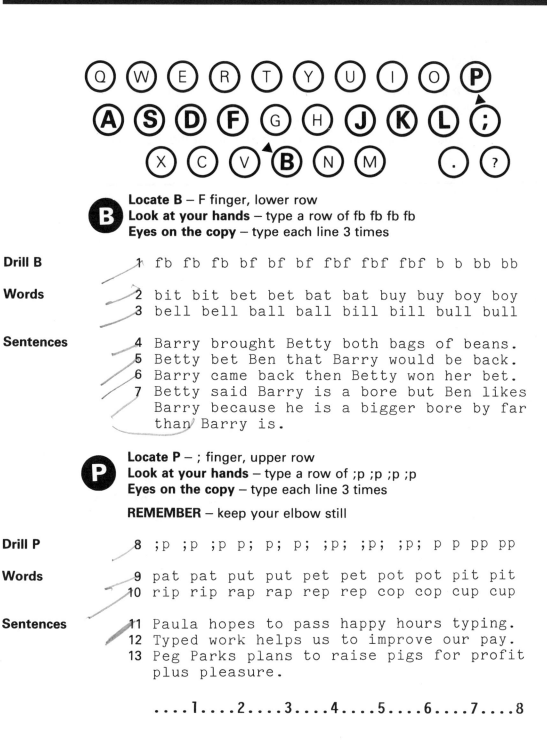

B Locate B – F finger, lower row
Look at your hands – type a row of fb fb fb fb
Eyes on the copy – type each line 3 times

Drill B

1 fb fb fb bf bf bf fbf fbf fbf b b bb bb

Words

2 bit bit bet bet bat bat buy buy boy boy
3 bell bell ball ball bill bill bull bull

Sentences

4 Barry brought Betty both bags of beans.
5 Betty bet Ben that Barry would be back.
6 Barry came back then Betty won her bet.
7 Betty said Barry is a bore but Ben likes
Barry because he is a bigger bore by far
than Barry is.

P Locate P – ; finger, upper row
Look at your hands – type a row of ;p ;p ;p ;p
Eyes on the copy – type each line 3 times

REMEMBER – keep your elbow still

Drill P

8 ;p ;p ;p p; p; p; ;p; ;p; ;p; p p pp pp

Words

9 pat pat put put pet pet pot pot pit pit
10 rip rip rap rap rep rep cop cop cup cup

Sentences

11 Paula hopes to pass happy hours typing.
12 Typed work helps us to improve our pay.
13 Peg Parks plans to raise pigs for profit
plus pleasure.

....1....2....3....4....5....6....7....8

Typing on cards

Typing the message

If there is a message to be typed on the card, it is typed on the other side from the address. Leave ½ inch margins.

If the company name and address have not been printed on the card, type this information on one line ½ inch from the top of the card. Leave half a line space below the address and type an unbroken line (with the underscore).

Vertical spacing will depend on the length of the message.

```
Eastview Hotel, Marine Parade, Brighton, Sussex
_____

11 October 1986

Please note our new telephone number effective
immediately is 0347 76776.

We look forward to having you visit our hotel
soon.
```

TASK 2

Prepare a post card with the following message to send to each of the companies listed. You are employed by Sarah's Boutique, 15 High Street, Meadows, Kent IK3 4RB. Use the current date.

Please send us a copy of your most recent catalogue. We are especially interested in your autumn and winter lines of sportswear and casual fashions.

Send to:

Greatex Ltd, 102 Whitechapel High St, London E1
Pringle of Scotland Ltd, 12a Savile Row, London W1

TASK 3

Prepare a post card to a car rental company inquiring the cost of renting a Ford Fiesta for a week. List your own name and address at the top. Use the current date. Refer to the telephone directory for a local car rental company.

Letter Z and ,

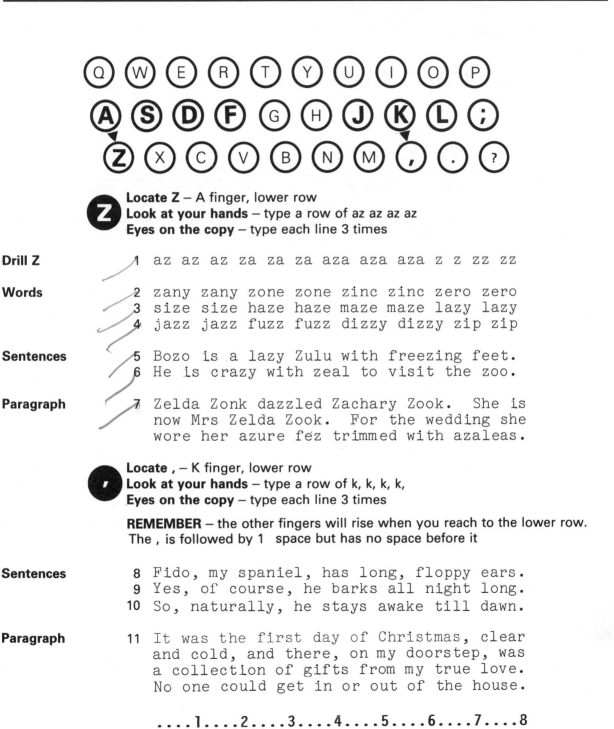

Z
Locate Z – A finger, lower row
Look at your hands – type a row of az az az az
Eyes on the copy – type each line 3 times

Drill Z
1 az az az za za za aza aza aza z z zz zz

Words
2 zany zany zone zone zinc zinc zero zero
3 size size haze haze maze maze lazy lazy
4 jazz jazz fuzz fuzz dizzy dizzy zip zip

Sentences
5 Bozo is a lazy Zulu with freezing feet.
6 He is crazy with zeal to visit the zoo.

Paragraph
7 Zelda Zonk dazzled Zachary Zook. She is
now Mrs Zelda Zook. For the wedding she
wore her azure fez trimmed with azaleas.

,
Locate , – K finger, lower row
Look at your hands – type a row of k, k, k, k,
Eyes on the copy – type each line 3 times

REMEMBER – the other fingers will rise when you reach to the lower row.
The , is followed by 1 space but has no space before it

Sentences
8 Fido, my spaniel, has long, floppy ears.
9 Yes, of course, he barks all night long.
10 So, naturally, he stays awake till dawn.

Paragraph
11 It was the first day of Christmas, clear
and cold, and there, on my doorstep, was
a collection of gifts from my true love.
No one could get in or out of the house.

....1....2....3....4....5....6....7....8

20

Section 3 Business applications

Office tasks; addressing cards

Office tasks

Speed in producing office documents depends as much on efficiency as it does on the speed of typing. By knowing each step thoroughly, you will be able to produce letters, memos, etc quickly and accurately the first time.

Every office task must be done correctly or it must be done again. For this reason, accuracy is the first priority. You will gain speed with experience, but you will always have to proofread carefully.

Cards

Announcements, invitations, reminders of appointments and short messages which are not private are often typed on cards of A6 size used landscape.

Addressing cards

If the card is to be sent by post, one side must be reserved for the address.

Roughly centre the address horizontally (you will easily be able to guess this with practice). Begin typing about half way down the card.

```
Miss Daisy Cameron
134 Mason Road
AINSWORTH
Devon   YJ4 7LK
```

TASK 1

Fold A4 paper to A6 size to represent post cards. Address cards to the following:

Autocrat Computers, 264 Preston Road, Harrow, Middx HA3 0P
Bug-Byte Software, 98-100 The Albany, Old Hall St, Liverpool L3 9ED
Chisholms Computer Supplies, 167 Drury Lane, London WC2B
Optimus, 1 Briset Street, London EC1M 5NP

Proficiency; typing by position

Proficiency

The only way to increase typing speed is to shorten the pauses between strokes.

The following sections are directly addressed to this skill. Pay close attention to the instructions and follow them exactly.

Typing by position

Efficiency is increased by eliminating unnecessary motions such as returning to the home row between strokes. Typing by position will shorten the pauses between strokes.

TASK 1

Type the word 'got' but instead of moving the F finger from G back to F, move directly to T as you are striking O. Type a line of 'got' this way.

TASK 2

Type this drill 3 times.

```
bug bug rot rot rig rig ham ham you you
```

TASK 3

Type this drill 3 times. Do not stop at the home row for strokes on the upper row followed by strokes on the lower row and vice versa.

```
mud mud nun nun bit bit may may cue cue
```

TASK 4

Type the following paragraph. Try to avoid returning to the home row between strokes. *(Note that a 'word' is taken as being an average word of 5 strokes in these word counts.)*

	Total words
This has definitely not been a day worth	8
remembering. My alarm clock chose today	16
to go on strike. The hot water ran only	24
halfway through my shower. My slices of	32
bread stuck in the toaster. To top all,	40
the handle broke off my cup as I started	48
to drink my tea. After that, things got	56
bad. The rest of the week is cancelled.	64

```
....1....2....3....4....5....6....7....8
```

In each task arrange the material in the form of a table. Centre each horizontally and vertically.

Choose an appropriate size and aspect of paper, margins, spacing between columns and line spacing to present the information effectively and attractively.

Select display techniques that will enhance the appearance of your work.

TASK 1

STAFF ASSIGNMENTS FOR SEPTEMBER

Shipping – Donna Stewart, Louise Kemp, Alice Dawson
Accounts – Yvonne Piper, Ellen Ross, Jean West

TASK 2

The following orders were received late:

Bookmasters – 50 copies CROSSWORD DICTIONARY
The Book Bin – 24 copies CHRISTMAS CAROLS FOR ALL
Carson's Books – 10 copies HISTORY IN THE MAKING

TASK 3

Expenses – Jane Latimer

		£
15 June	lunch	4.75
16 June	taxi	2.80
18 June	postage	.95
		£8.50

TASK 4

Contents

Letters	3
Tabulations	15
Invoices	27
Statements	32
Minutes	36

Combinations of letters; rhythm

Combinations of letters

Easy and frequent combinations of letters can be typed very quickly as units. TH, for example, is typed as a unit rather than as T and then H.

Other combinations are slower to type as they must be typed letter by letter.

Break words and numbers into easy combinations wherever possible.

Type these examples several times. You may find that you can type some 3-letter combinations instead of 2-letter.

```
starfish        st ar fi sh
mahogany        ma ho ga ny
residential     re si den ti al
alphabetical    al ph ab et ic al
```

Rhythm

Achieve a flowing rhythm in typing in order to increase speed, improve keyboard control and promote fluency.

Rhythm in typing should be flowing. Type the easy combinations quickly but slow down for the letter by letter combinations.

Type this paragraph 3 times, breaking the words into easy combinations of letters.

	Total words
The modern typewriter is operated with a	8
speed and efficiency developed by energy	16
and concentration on the techniques that	24
must be mastered by competent operators.	32

```
....1....2....3....4....5....6....7....8
```

Centring a table

Horizontal centring of a table

To centre a table it is only necessary to find the left margin by backspacing from the centrepoint.

Use a suitable size and aspect of paper – the method is always the same.

```
bread      butter
fish       chips
bacon      eggs
coffee     toast
```

TASK 1

Follow these steps. There are 4 spaces between the columns.

1 Zero your margins.
2 Clear all tab stops.
3 Move to the midpoint.
4 Backspace once for each 2 letters and spaces.

   co ff ee ## ## bu tt er

5 Set left margin.
6 Set a tab stop.
7 Type the table.

TASK 2

Centre the following table horizontally. Leave 6 spaces between the columns.

```
tulips        chestnut
roses         oak
asters        elm
daffodils     cedar
pansies       pine
```

Vertical centring of a table

Tables are often centred vertically. Use the same procedure as you use for centring an announcement.

Compose It Yourself

Type an attractive table using the information given. Use a variety of display techniques and choose a suitable size and aspect of paper.

Choose an appropriate main heading and use column headings where required for clarity.

TASK

Prepare a holiday schedule for the staff. From 1 – 15 July Nancy Howard, John Harker, Brenda Simmons and Ted Anderson will be off. From 15 – 29 July Bob Brewer, Jack Barton, Carl Davis and Catherine Hughes will be off.

Chaining

Frequently typed groups of letters have very short pauses between the letters. The group becomes a single response known as a **chain**. The more chains the typist has in his/her repertoire, the faster and more accurately he/she will type.

Most chains have 2 letters although, as you gain more typing experience, you will develop some 3 and 4 letter chains.

In order to identify those chains you have not mastered, type the following lines quickly. Do not repeat any lines; type the exercise just as it appears and group the letters in 2-letter chains.

When you have finished, note those chains over which you hesitated or which you typed wrong, then proceed to the corrective drill for each (pages 40–4). Double letter drills are on page 46.

Diagnostic chaining drills

1	able	acre	afar	also	change	braise	amount
2	flag	that	draw	play	draper	trauma	blazer
3	east	ecru	edge	free	admire	either	ascent
4	else	stem	even	exit	eulogy	ignite	client
5	epic	whet	grew	skid	inborn	spirit	island
6	trim	grip	oath	blob	octave	brogue	stolen
7	prod	from	once	crop	closet	shower	oyster
8	oven	bark	bike	body	become	bubble	future
9	were	pack	clan	cuff	dinner	dagger	gopher
10	cyst	fine	desk	dolt	design	gutter	jester
11	duty	fall	fold	gaze	hobble	jiggle	jovial
12	girl	glee	hart	hemp	narrow	notice	peddle
13	hilt	hulk	jazz	jump	quarto	scrape	summer
14	knew	life	moss	mute	switch	twelve	vacant
15	null	pine	posy	puma	supply	volume	wallet
16	rack	word	ripe	yarn	yellow	wrench	rotate
17	harp	save	slim	smog	snooze	wilted	escape
18	axis	avid	byte	kiss	origin	cinema	opiate

Confused letters

If you frequently confuse 2 letters eg typing an E instead of an I, you will find drills for the most commonly confused letters on page 39.

Column and main headings; arranging material for typing

Column headings

The longest item may be the heading or an item within the column. Treat the heading as part of the column. Type Task 1 on A5 landscape; 1½ inch left margin; 5 spaces between columns.

TASK 1

Surname	Christian Name	Date of Birth
Henderson	Dennis	15 May 1962
Bayer	Anthony	30 April 1964

Main headings

Tables are always identified by a main heading. When at work, if none is provided, choose it yourself. Leave 2 lines of clear space after the main heading. Type Task 2 with 2½ inch left margin. Choose a suitable size and aspect of the paper.

TASK 2

LOCAL FLORA AND FAUNA

birds	trees	flowers
sparrow	elm	lily
finch	fir	poppy

TASK 3

Choose a main title and type this table. Leave 4 spaces between columns and set a left margin of 2 inches.

Subject	Time	Instructor
Flute	10:15 am	Peters
Viola	11:45 am	Brown

Arranging material for typing

Sometimes material is presented column by column instead of in the order you will type it. Type the following material in an attractive table.

TASK 1

Main heading SCHOOL CLUBS
1st column Squash, Track, Swimming
2nd column Choir, Sketching, Drama
3rd column First Aid, Referees, Volunteers

Common words

These words make up a major part of those you will type so you will notice a significant improvement in speed as you master them.
   Type smoothly and quickly until you come to a difficult word or you make an error. Type the word 3 or 4 times, until it is smooth and easy, then proceed with the drill.

1 am an as at be by do go he if is in two
  it me my no of on or so to up us we yes

2 all and any are but can day end did far
  for get got had has her him his how its

3 let man may men new nor not now off old
  one our out put saw say see she the too

4 also back been busy call came city come
  does done down easy even ever find from

5 full give goes good have head here home
  hope hour into just keep know last left

6 less life like long look lost love made
  make many miss more most move much must

7 near need next once only over part past
  plan quit real rest rush said seem sell

8 send sent sign some stop such suit sure
  take tell than that them then they this

9 time true turn upon very want well went
  were what when will with work year your

10 about after again alone being below try
   clear could every extra first going use

11 great heard light never often order was
   other price quick quiet quite reply way

12 right round shall start still thank who
   their there these thing think those why

13 truly under until usual watch where yet
   which while world would write yours you

Spacing between columns

The same number of spaces is usually left between columns to give a balanced appearance.

It is common practice to leave at least 3 spaces but no more than 6 spaces between columns; if there are more than 6 the eye tends to wander and if there are fewer than 3 the work looks crowded. You will learn to judge the best layout.

TASK 1

For the following tasks use A4 paper portrait. Begin 1 inch from the top of the paper and leave 3 lines of clear space after each task.

Arrange the material below in 3 columns leaving 4 spaces between the columns. Set the left margin at 15 and clear all tab stops before you begin.

A column is as wide as the longest item in the column. When making the tab settings, tap the space bar once for each letter of the longest word in each column, add 4 spaces, then set your tab. Do the same for the second tab setting.

The longest item is underlined for you.

```
Paris          Rome           Berlin
Washington     Tokyo          Ottawa
Madrid         London         Amsterdam
```

Your tab stops should be set at 29 and 39. Now type the table.

TASK 2

Experiment with different spacing between columns and decide which you prefer. Change the left margin, too. Try settings of 20 and 25. Which do you think looks best?

TASK 3

Try these examples yourself. Choose attractive spacing.

Line 1:   Monday, _Tuesday,_ _Wednesday_

Line 2:   _Thursday,_ Friday, Saturday

TASK 4

Type the following in 3 columns. Set the left margin at 15 and choose attractive spacing between columns.

Ella Maxwell, secretary, 366 4455 / Donna Perkins, accountant, 343 8987 / Carol Gordon, receptionist, 388 9009 / Debbie Taylor, typist, 876 3564

TASK 5

Type the following material in columns. Decide the number of columns and the settings you will use.

Flour, salt, milk, sugar, eggs, cheese, bacon, noodles, pepper, tomatoes, celery, lettuce

Numbers; numbers 3 and 4

Numbers

A new home row is used for typing numbers.

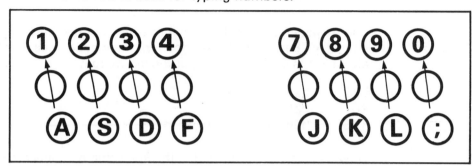

Locate 3 and 4 – move your hands to the number row
Look at your hands – type a row of 34 34 34 34
                          type a row of 43 43 43 43
Eyes on the copy – type each line 3 times

Drill

1   34 34 34 43 43 43 33 33 44 44 34 3 4 3 4
2   43 34 43 34 3 3 4 4 33 33 44 44 43 34 43

Long numbers

Type long numbers in easy 2-key chains just as you type long words.

3   3344 4433 3443 4334 343344 434334 433434

When typing numbers and words in the same sentence, move the whole hand up to the 4th row to type the numbers then return to the home row. With practice you will be able to reach only 1 finger up if you need to type just 1 number.

Sentences

4   I have read 33 or 34 pages in chapter 3.
5   The 4 of them live at 44 Elm in Flat 43.

Paragraph

6   On 4 May, I will ring 3 Aces Motors; the number is 334 4334. The amount shown on the invoice is 4 pounds; I owe 3 pounds.

Speed

7   This work is very easy for me to do now.
8   You never know who you are going to see.

    ....1....2....3....4....5....6....7....8

Tabulating for columns

You should use the tab bar/key to type columns quickly, typing the first line in each column, then the next, and so on.

TASK 1

Use A4 paper portrait. Clear all tab stops. Set the left margin at 10 and a tab stop at 30. Begin 1 inch from the top of the paper. Leave 3 lines of clear space after each task. Begin typing at the left margin.

```
100     (tabulate)     1000
200     (tabulate)     2000
300     (tabulate)     3000
```

TASK 2

Now try 3 columns. Notice that the first column begins at the margin so to type 3 columns, 2 tab stops are needed.
    Set the left margin at 10 and tab stops at 30 and 50. Type:

```
Sam     (tabulate)     Joe     (tabulate)     Ida
Ken     (tabulate)     Bob     (tabulate)     Sue
Ted     (tabulate)     Gus     (tabulate)     Pat
```

TASK 3

Set the left margin at 10 and tab stops at 20, 30 and 40. Type each line and be sure to tabulate after each item you type.

Line 1:   red, pink, yellow, orange
Line 2:   blue, green, aqua, lime
Line 3:   brown, beige, black, grey

It should look like this:

```
red          pink          yellow          orange
blue         green         aqua            lime
brown        beige         black           grey
```

TASK 4

Clear all tab stops and make these settings: left margin 20, tab stops at 35 and 50. List in 3 columns the following items:

Line 1 – starter, soup, fish/Line 2 – salad, main course, dessert/Line 3 – cheese, coffee, biscuits

Numbers 7 and 8

IMPORTANT Do not neglect speed and accuracy practice. During each session you should type at least one speed and accuracy passage. Instructions and practice passages are on pages 35–8.

Locate 7 and 8 – move your hands to the number row
Look at your hands – type a row of 78 78 78 78
  type a row of 87 87 87 87
Eyes on the copy – type each line 3 times

Drill 7 8

```
1  78  78  87  87  77  77  88  88  7  8  7  8  78  88  77
2  78  78  87  87  7  7  8  8  77  77  88  88  77  78  88
3  74  73  47  37  84  83  48  38  78  87  88  3  4  7  8
```

Longer numbers

```
4  7873  3734  4483  4873  8477  3843  3347  74883
5  8374  7348  8837  7784  4378  4744  8738  34748
```

Sentences

```
6  Bring 78 pens, 87 pencils and 88 papers.
7  I saw 77 wrens and 38 owls from the 747.
```

Paragraph

```
8  My appointment is at 4 pm on 7 March.  I
   tried to arrange it for 3 pm on the 8th,
   but 77 or 78 people all wanted that time
   so 73 of us changed.  My file No is 4337
   so I must go to Room 83 in Building A73.
```

Speed

```
9   He knows he will grow in skill each day.
10  Let go of the key the instant it is hit.
```

```
....1....2....3....4....5....6....7....8
```

Type this announcement centring each line horizontally and the whole announcement vertically. Be sure to allow for decorative lines when calculating the vertical placement. Note that many of the symbols can be used for decorative lines.

*

STUDENTS

* *

PICNIC

* * *

SUNDAY

* *

RIVERSIDE PARK

*

Apply Your Skill

Experiment with display techniques to set up and type these notices.
   Choose a suitable size and aspect of paper for each. Arrange the material clearly and attractively.

1 Red Cross Blood Donor Clinic   Monday 19 May
  Red Cross House 46 Temple Road   9 am – 9 pm
  Give the Gift of Life

2 Due to unforseen circumstances Flower Show
  Friday, 9 April Cancelled   St. Mary's Church
  Ticket refunds at the church office.

Compose It Yourself

Use any display techniques to type attractive notices.

1 *Prepare a notice advertising your services as a typist, available to type theses, correspondence, statistical reports, financial statements and summaries. State that your rates are reasonable and that you will pick up and deliver. Include your name and telephone number.*

2 *The Valley College of Music are presenting the pop group, Thunderbolt, in concert at the Valley Auditorium for 3 nights starting Thursday, 15 April. Tickets are £2 each for all seats. Type a notice to advertise the concert. Consider the audience in choosing the words you will use.*

Numbers 1 and 2

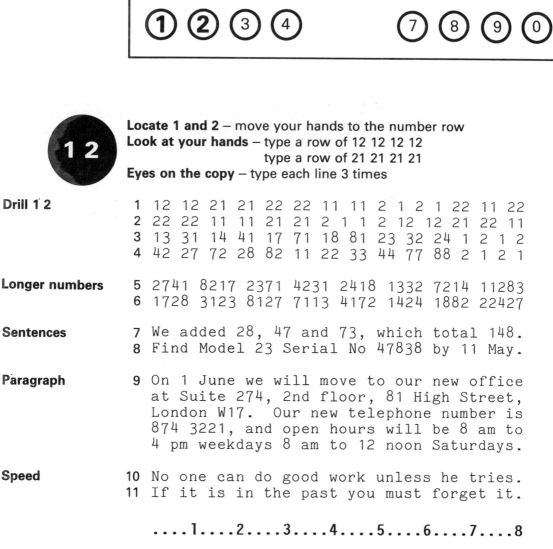

① ② ③ ④   ⑦ ⑧ ⑨ ⓪

Locate 1 and 2 – move your hands to the number row
Look at your hands – type a row of 12 12 12 12
         type a row of 21 21 21 21
Eyes on the copy – type each line 3 times

Drill 1 2

1 12 12 21 21 22 22 11 11 2 1 2 1 22 11 22
2 22 22 11 11 21 21 2 1 1 2 12 12 21 22 11
3 13 31 14 41 17 71 18 81 23 32 24 1 2 1 2
4 42 27 72 28 82 11 22 33 44 77 88 2 1 2 1

Longer numbers

5 2741 8217 2371 4231 2418 1332 7214 11283
6 1728 3123 8127 7113 4172 1424 1882 22427

Sentences

7 We added 28, 47 and 73, which total 148.
8 Find Model 23 Serial No 47838 by 11 May.

Paragraph

9 On 1 June we will move to our new office
   at Suite 274, 2nd floor, 81 High Street,
   London W17. Our new telephone number is
   874 3221, and open hours will be 8 am to
   4 pm weekdays 8 am to 12 noon Saturdays.

Speed

10 No one can do good work unless he tries.
11 If it is in the past you must forget it.

    ....1....2....3....4....5....6....7....8

Varying the line spacing

Leaving extra lines of clear space gives importance to certain material.

```
ROTARY CLUB
Regular Meeting for February

CANCELLED

Next Meeting in March
Let's have a full turnout
```

Leader dots

Leader dots lead the eye across the page. They may be closed (no spaces between) or open (one or more spaces between single or grouped dots).
Leave a space at each end of a row of leader dots.

```
Green Salad ..................... Monday
```

Dots must line up vertically.

```
.  .  .  .  .         ...  ...  ...  ...

.  .  .  .  .         ...  ...  ...  ...
```

Decorative lines and borders

Lines can be typed with symbols as well as with the underscore.

```
. . . . . . . . . .    - - - - - - - - - -    + + + + + + + + + +    # # # # # # # #

= = = = = = = = = =    ! ! ! ! ! ! ! ! ! !    " " " " " " " " " " "    * * * * * * * * * *
```

TASK 1

Type this schedule on A5 portrait using leader dots to connect the 2 columns. Centre horizontally and vertically.

```
PRACTICE SCHEDULE

Team 1 ............ Monday

Team 2 ............ Tuesday

Team 3 ............ Wednesday
```

Numbers 9 and 0

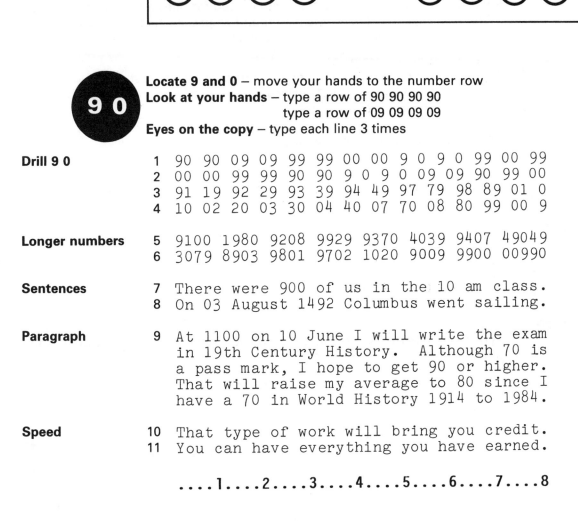

① ② ③ ④   ⑦ ⑧ **⑨** **⓪**

9 0

Locate 9 and 0 – move your hands to the number row
Look at your hands – type a row of 90 90 90 90
                              type a row of 09 09 09 09
Eyes on the copy – type each line 3 times

Drill 9 0

1 90 90 09 09 99 99 00 00 9 0 9 0 99 00 99
2 00 00 99 99 90 90 9 0 9 0 09 09 90 99 00
3 91 19 92 29 93 39 94 49 97 79 98 89 01 0
4 10 02 20 03 30 04 40 07 70 08 80 99 00 9

Longer numbers

5 9100 1980 9208 9929 9370 4039 9407 49049
6 3079 8903 9801 9702 1020 9009 9900 00990

Sentences

7 There were 900 of us in the 10 am class.
8 On 03 August 1492 Columbus went sailing.

Paragraph

9 At 1100 on 10 June I will write the exam
   in 19th Century History. Although 70 is
   a pass mark, I hope to get 90 or higher.
   That will raise my average to 80 since I
   have a 70 in World History 1914 to 1984.

Speed

10 That type of work will bring you credit.
11 You can have everything you have earned.

....1....2....3....4....5....6....7....8

Display techniques

A number of different devices can be used to emphasise certain parts of text or an announcement.

Spaced capitals

S P A C E D   C A P I T A L S   are often used for titles and main headings. There is a space between each letter and 3 spaces between words.
To centre a heading using spaced capitals:

1 Move to the centre point.
2 Backspace once for each letter and space except the last one.
3 Type the heading, leaving 1 space between each letter and 3 spaces between words.

TASK 1

Centre these titles using spaced capitals.

```
NIGHT SOUNDS
TOMORROW NEVER CAME
```

Underlining

Except for titles and main headings, underlining is usually used with initial capitals. Underlining closed capitals tends to look cluttered and loses the effectiveness of the closed capitals.

Emboldening

Type a second time over the first example to darken the type and make it stand out.

```
immediately          immediately
```

Combining upper and upper and lower case

Varying the case within a line will tend to emphasise both parts.

```
Adorable PET SNAKE needs a NEW BELL.
```

TASK 2

Type the following using an appropriate display technique to highlight the most important part of each line.

```
Meet me at 6 pm for dinner.
Classes begin 15 September.
```

Numbers 5 and 6

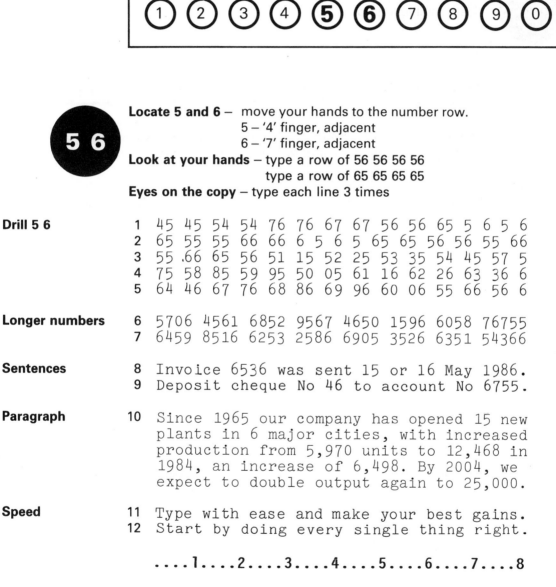

① ② ③ ④ **⑤** **⑥** ⑦ ⑧ ⑨ ⓪

5 6

Locate 5 and 6 – move your hands to the number row.
    5 – '4' finger, adjacent
    6 – '7' finger, adjacent
Look at your hands – type a row of 56 56 56 56
         type a row of 65 65 65 65
Eyes on the copy – type each line 3 times

Drill 5 6

1 45 45 54 54 76 76 67 67 56 56 65 5 6 5 6
2 65 55 55 66 66 6 5 6 5 65 65 56 56 55 66
3 55 .66 65 56 51 15 52 25 53 35 54 45 57 5
4 75 58 85 59 95 50 05 61 16 62 26 63 36 6
5 64 46 67 76 68 86 69 96 60 06 55 66 56 6

Longer numbers

6 5706 4561 6852 9567 4650 1596 6058 76755
7 6459 8516 6253 2586 6905 3526 6351 54366

Sentences

8 Invoice 6536 was sent 15 or 16 May 1986.
9 Deposit cheque No 46 to account No 6755.

Paragraph

10 Since 1965 our company has opened 15 new
     plants in 6 major cities, with increased
     production from 5,970 units to 12,468 in
     1984, an increase of 6,498. By 2004, we
     expect to double output again to 25,000.

Speed

11 Type with ease and make your best gains.
12 Start by doing every single thing right.

    ....1....2....3....4....5....6....7....8

You will often be required to 'put up a notice about . . .' and you will be responsible for the wording and layout yourself. Try the following tasks to test your skill.

Using the information given, first draft, then type the notices. Strive for clarity and attractive appearance. Choose an appropriate size and aspect of the paper. Use capital letters for emphasis.

TASK 1   *The winner of the shorthand contest was Natalie Parker, who achieved a speed of 180 wpm.*

TASK 2   *The House of Fashion at 213 Park Gardens is having an anniversary sale. It starts Monday, 9 October at 10 am and there will be reductions of up to 50%*

Centring each line

More formal announcements and invitations are usually centred line by line.

TASK 3

BRIDGEWAY COMPUTERS

request the pleasure of your company

at the opening of their new office

62 Drummond Road

3 pm, Tuesday, 6 March

RSVP

TASK 4

The cafeteria special lunch changes every day. Here is today's special — cream of celery soup, cucumber salad, grilled pork cutlets, roast potatoes, steamed carrots, creme caramel.

Review numbers

TASK 1   Set the left margin at 15 and copy this paragraph line for line as it appears.

The general office is open 5 days a week from 0900
to 1700. Most departments close for lunch from 1100
to 1200, 1200 to 1300 or 1300 to 1400. Telephone
enquiries are handled evenings and weekends; ring
356 8792 or 985 4480.

TASK 2   Set the left margin at 20 and type the following passage. Blocked paragraphs
begin at the left margin and have one line space between them.

I had travelled 200 km that Saturday and arrived at
1800 hrs, just in time to change into my new outfit
for the engagement party. My cousin had collected
me at the station and we hurried to her flat.

I looked lovely, I thought, as I put on the finishing
touches. Then I opened the box with my new shoes.
They were both for the right foot. I wear size 7 and
my cousin wears size 4.

I was the only one at the party wearing plimsolls.

TASK 3   Set the left margin at 10 pica or 20 elite and type the following passage line
for line. Remember to leave a line of clear space between the paragraphs.

Most of the students are 15 or 16 years old and have studied
18th century poetry for at least 2 years. Each term there
were at least 2 essays assigned, each of them 25 pages long
and requiring an analysis of 8 poems.

The next course in the series will be Literature since 1920
and will require the reading of 4 novels, each 300 to 400
pages long. Since the course is 12 weeks, students will be
reading about 200 pages a week or 40 to 50 pages a day. It
is suggested that no more than 2 other courses be taken
concurrently.

Display — Vertical centring

Both pica and elite have 6 lines to the vertical inch. Note the number of vertical line spaces in these portrait and landscape sizes:

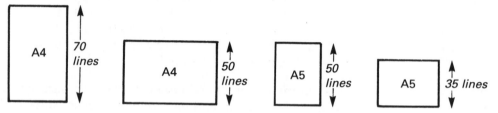

To centre vertically:

1   Count the number of lines that will be used for typing the material.
2   Subtract that number from the total available.
3   Divide the remainder equally between the top and bottom margins.
4   Begin typing on the *next* line down.

Should there be a fraction in the remainder, ignore it, as the extra line of clear space is left at the bottom.

```
Line 1  ANNOUNCEMENT
     2
     3  Starting on Monday, 11 May, this shop will be open
     4
     5  Monday to Saturday from 10 am till 6 pm.
```

TASK 1

This announcement will require 5 lines of vertical space.
   On A5 portrait the calculations for spacing are as follows:

Available lines = 50
Required   =   5

Available space = 45 ÷ 2 = 22 lines for top margin

Typing begins line 23.

Type the announcement. Left margin 10 pica, 12 elite.

TASK 2

Calculate the vertical spacing for the same announcement on A5 landscape, A4 portrait and A4 landscape.

TASK 3

Centre the following horizontally and vertically on A5 landscape.

FOR SALE
SKI BOOTS, SIZE 6, GOOD CONDITION
239 7116 after 7 pm

Symbols

Nearly all symbols are upper case characters and vary in position from one machine to another. Not all symbols appear on all machines.

Use the correct finger for symbols above the numbers. For symbols on the right of the keyboard, use the little finger of the right hand.

Type each example 3 times.

: The colon introduces a list and is followed by 1 space.

Buy: paper, pens, pencils, envelopes.
Try: honey, syrup, sugar, molasses.

/ The solidus is used in numbers and in fractions. It has no space before or after it.

More than 2/3 of the members attended.

Form A/238 is required with payment.

" Quotation marks are used for direct quotations. There is no space between them and the material they enclose.

Sharon said, "I have your ticket."

"Thank you," he replied.

& The ampersand is a word and has a space before and after it.

Jenny works for Clark & Company.
P & O means Pacific and Orient.

- The hyphen joins words together and uses the space between them.
It also joins words broken by line length. Type the hyphen only on the first line. The hyphen with a space before and after it constitutes the dash.

My sister-in-law went to Italy.

Make sure that the whole depart-
ment is informed.
Sam - I met him last week - rang me.
Early in the day - about 0800 - he rang

The underscore is used for underlining. It strikes the paper under the letter. Do not confuse the underscore with the hyphen. A row of hyphens will go through the centre of the word instead of underlining it.

Read The Jungle Book for us.

Do it now.

Shift lock Use the shift lock with the underscore, or to type in capitals.

BASIC TYPING SKILLS

This symbol used before numbers means number. Used after a letter it means sharp (music).

Policy #32643 expires 31 July.

Transpose the music to the key of C#.

Display — horizontal centring

The term 'display' is used to describe typed material which does not follow set typing conventions (rules), as letters do, but which needs to be set out (displayed) attractively on the page.

Material to be displayed can either have every line centred (**centred style**) or have all lines beginning at the same point (**blocked style**).

Horizontal centring — blocked style

Centre display pieces horizontally so that the longest line is centred. Use suitable size and aspect of paper — the method is always the same.

```
PIANO LESSONS

Children and Adults

Reasonable Rates

Marilyn Van Osterland
```

TASK 1

Follow these steps to type the above display piece.

1 Move the margins out to the ends of the scale, ie, zero your margins.
2 Move to the centre point.
3 Operate the backspace once for every 2 characters in the longest line — Ma ri ly n# Va n# Os te rl an.
4 Set the left margin at the point at which you stopped backspacing.
5 Type the announcement. All lines will begin at the left margin.

TASK 2

Centre this notice horizontally (blocked style) on A5 portrait.

```
SUMMER SALE OF FASHION APPAREL

Monica's Boutique, 33 Garden Grove Court

Begins Monday, 23 July, 10 am

Everything in the shop reduced by 25%
```

TASK 3

Retype on A5 landscape. Which do you think looks more attractive?

$ **or** **£**	There is no space between the symbol and the amount of money.	The totals are £103.70 and $103.70

In figures the decimal points are aligned and the £ and $ is typed over the first digit and before the total.

The double underscore is used below columns of figures. Use the variable line spacer to type the second line. Note the space to be left above and below the lines for the total.

```
£              $
107.00         107.00
   .65            .65
 96.05          96.05
————————       ————————

£103.70        $103.70

════════       ════════
```

% There is no space between the number and per cent.

All stock is reduced 50%.

More than 80% of the staff were there.

* The asterisk is used for footnotes or decoration.

*revised annually

DINNER MENU

() Like quotation marks, there is no space between the brackets and the material they enclose.

My car (a sports model) is blue.

Bill (my oldest brother) plays football.

½ A fraction that is on the keyboard has no space before it if it is typed with a whole number.

Add 1½ cups of sugar to 4½ cups of milk.

We waited 2½ hours for the train.

' The apostrophe represents letters omitted in contractions and is also used in possessives. It has no space before or after it unless it is used as a plural possessive (boys' shoes).

Carol's shoes are too tight.

Ladies' Wear is now on the 3rd floor.

! The apostrophe is also used to form the exclamation mark if there is not one on the keyboard. Type ' then backspace and type . directly below it. The exclamation mark is followed by 2 spaces.

Hurry! We're late!

Hey! Cheers! Well done! We won!

@ This symbol means 'at' and shows the unit price for an item.

Buy 12 copies @ £3.50.

We sold 50 shares @ £100.

Centring a paragraph heading

Use the midpoint of the longest line in a paragraph to centre the heading. Find the midpoint of a line by tapping the space bar once for every 2 letters in the line.

TASK 1

Type the following paragraph on A4 portrait line for line as it appears. Centre the heading as shown. Set the left margin at 20 pica, 24 elite.

```
                    PUNCTUALITY

Punctuality is said to be the courtesy of kings.  It
shows respect for the value of time, especially the
time of the person granting the interview.
```

TASK 2

Centre the heading TELEPHONE MANNERS then type the paragraph below. Set your left margin at 20 pica or 24 elite and copy line for line.

```
Answer the telephone with a smile and your voice will
carry this pleasant message to the caller.  If the
caller wishes to speak to someone who is not available
at present, ask if you may take a message.
```

TASK 3

Choose a suitable title for the following passage. Centre it and type the paragraph. Set margins 20 and 62 for pica, 24 and 76 elite.

```
Dress suitably for your office job.  Be comfortable
but not sloppy, fashionable but not avant-garde.  Keep
jewellery tailored in style and wear your hair in a
style that requires a minimum of attention.
```

TASK 4

Type the following paragraph on A4 portrait. Set margins at 20 and 62 pica or 24 and 76 elite. Choose and centre an appropriate heading.

Every day there are more opportunities for well-trained workers. Even though occupations have changed a great deal in the last 30 years, the labour force still requires entry level workers to fill the spaces as well as meet the demands of expansion.

Punctuation; abbreviations; measurement; numbers and figures

Punctuation

'Open' punctuation, where full stops are *not* typed after abbreviations (eg Mr B Carr), is generally preferable to 'full' punctuation, where full stops *are* typed after abbreviations (eg Mr. B. Carr).

In open punctuation, full stops are only used where the abbreviation is the last word in the sentence or there could be confusion or ambiguity by their omission.

Consistency of punctuation, open or full, must be maintained throughout the document. Type the following examples.

TASK 1

```
Mrs J Carter has an appointment at IBM at 3 pm not 10 am.
Claim No 7885 was adjudicated by Mr T Bell at 1400 hours.
```

Manuscript abbreviations

Manuscript draft abbreviations must be typed in full.

sh	shall	wd	would	yr	year
shd	should	w	with	yr	your
wh	which	wl	will	dr	dear

Measurement

In typing measurement, remember that a number is a word on its own and therefore has a space before and after it. Abbreviations of units of measurement have neither a full stop following nor an 's' in the plural form. Dimensions often use 'x' instead of 'by'. Type the following examples.

TASK 2

```
The legal speed limit is 100 km per hour.
Cutting a lawn 60 m x 80 m takes at least 2 hours.
```

Numbers and figures

Type all numbers as figures unless the number begins a sentence or is the number one standing alone in the text. Type the paragraph below.

TASK 3

```
Five of us went to 20 or 30 shops to look for
size 4 shoes.  We found one shop that had
sizes 4½ and 5 but not size 4.
```

Typing headings; centring words

Typing headings

A heading may be blocked (begin at the left margin) or centred.

**Centred headings
– finding the
centre point**

Horizontal centring is calculated from the centre point of a page. With the left-hand edge of the paper at 0, the centre point on any paper is half the space number of the right-hand edge.

The most common centre points are shown in the table.

Paper	Aspect	Characters	Centre point
A4	portrait	82 pica 100 elite	41 pica 50 elite
A4	landscape	118 pica 141 elite	59 pica 70 elite
A5	portrait	59 pica 70 elite	29 pica 35 elite
A5	landscape	82 pica 100 elite	41 pica 50 elite

Horizontally centring a word

From the centre point, backspace once for each 2 letters. Starting at the beginning of the word, say the letters to yourself in pairs.

TASK 1

To centre TYPIST, move to the centre point and backspace once for each pair of letters.

TY (*backspace*) PI (*backspace*) ST (*backspace*)

Begin typing at the point at which you stopped backspacing.

TASK 2

If the word has an odd number of letters, ignore any letter that is left over. Do not backspace for it. Centre TYPEWRITING.

TY PE WR IT IN

Centring 2 or more words

To centre LEARNING TO TYPE, consider a space to be a letter when you backspace.

TASK 3

LE AR NI NG #T O# TY PE

TASK 4

Centre each of the following in closed capitals, ie capitals with no spaces between them, on A5 paper portrait.

COMPUTERS
WORD PROCESSING

Money in continuous matter; consolidation

Money in continuous matter

In typing sums of money there are alternatives but the style must be kept consistent within the piece of work.

Less than £1   £0.50, 50p, 50 pence or fifty pence
£1 or more   round numbers of pounds – £50 or £50.00 or fifty pounds
                    mixed pounds and pence – £50.10 is always used
                    millions of pounds – £50m or £50,000,000 or £50 000 000 or
                    £50 million or fifty million pounds

TASK 4

Type these examples.

The lunch cost four pounds plus fifty pence tip.

The lunch cost £4 plus 50p tip.

The lunch cost £4.00 plus £0.50 tip.

Consolidation

The following tasks will consolidate your skill and test your understanding and ability to apply the skills you have learned.

Type each of the following passages line for line on A4 paper. Set the left margin at 10.

TASK 1

Mrs Della R Belton wl call to see Mr Thomson about 3 pm. She wd like to review her policy No 61665, wch expires 30 June this yr. Her present coverage is £50,000. She has been a client for over 20 yr and we shd extend her every courtesy.

TASK 2

Yr order No 6293 for 2 copies of HARPER'S FOLLY has been passed to our shipping dept. Our minimum invoicing is for £10 and the total cost of yr order is £6.64, so this amount will be invoiced w yr next order.

Numbering paragraphs

Paragraph numbers (or letters) are typed at the left margin and are followed by 2 spaces.

Set a tab stop for the paragraphs. Some machines have tab stops which cannot be moved. If you have preset tab stops on your machine, use the first stop.

TASK 4

Type the following on A5 landscape with 1½ inch left margin. Leave 2 lines of clear space after the heading.

```
A NUTRITIOUS BREAKFAST


1   Include a high protein food.  Eggs, milk, meat,
    fish and cheese are all good sources of protein.

2   Carbohydrates are necessary.  Good sources are
    cereals and bread.

3   Fat is required and is usually provided by the
    butter on toast, fat content of egg yolk or
    butterfat in milk or cream.

4   Vitamins are found in fruits and vegetables.
```

TASK 5

Type a finished copy.

THE EMPLOYMENT INTERVIEW

1. Dress conservatively. A suit or tailored dress is most appropriate.
2. Be prompt. Arrive 5 minutes before the appointed time.
3. Be prepared. Bring all certificates and documents that may be required.
4. Show more interest in the job than in the wages.

Improving speed and accuracy

Timings

Timings measure progress, force speed and identify weaknesses.

Measuring progress

In using a timing to measure progress, type at a speed that will assure good keyboard control. If you make more than 1 error per minute, slow down.

Forcing speed

Forcing the stroking rate increases speed by eliminating unnecessary finger motions.

Identifying weaknesses

Under timing conditions, weaknesses and hesitations soon become obvious and can be corrected.

Taking a timing for measurement

- Timings should be double spaced for ease in reading and correcting.
- Leave margins of at least 1 inch.
- Begin to type when you are given the signal but do not race. Start to type at a moderate pace and build your rate as you go along.
- If you feel nervous and pressured, slow down rather than try to speed up.
- Stop exactly on the signal, even if you are in the middle of a word.

Gross rate

Divide the total number of words you typed by the number of minutes.
(5 strokes = 1 word)

Allowance for errors

In marking timings, circle each word with an error in it. The allowance for errors is 1 error per minute plus 1 overall. Therefore:

1-minute timing – 2 errors	3-minute timing – 4 errors
2-minute timing – 3 errors	5-minute timing – 6 errors

Calculate the number of words typed up to the 'fatal error', which for a 1 minute timing is the 3rd error, for a 2 minute timing is the 4th error, for a 3 minute timing is the 5th error and for a 5 minute timing is the 7th error. Disregard anything typed after the fatal error is reached.

Net rate

Divide the number of words (up to the fatal error) by the number of minutes you typed. The result is your net rate.

Tabulating; indenting paragraphs

Tabulating

The tabulator on your machine sets points to the right of the left-hand margin at which the carriage will stop.

Some applications are the indenting of paragraphs and the layout of material in columns.

TASK 1

Follow the instructions below to set tab stops at 20, 40, 55 and 60.

Clearing the tab   Move to the end of the typing line and depress the tab clear key, which may be labelled clear, tab clear, –, or tab –. Hold this key down as you return the carriage. That will remove all stops.

Setting a tab stop   Move to the space at which you wish to set a tab stop and depress the tab set key, which may be labelled set, tab set, +, or tab +. You can set as many stops as you need.

Tabulating   To move the carriage to a stop that has been set, press the tabulator, which may be a key or a bar. If your machine is a manual, you must hold the tabulator down until the carriage stops. An electric machine needs only a tap of the key.

Indenting paragraphs

Paragraphs are sometimes indented 5 spaces.

TASK 2

Type these paragraphs, indenting the paragraphs.

```
     More and more occupations require the
use of typing or at least a knowledge of
typing.
     A student taking a computer course will
find that being able to type frees his mind
for the specific learning he requires.
```

TASK 3

a   Type the paragraphs below. Indent the paragraphs.
b   Type the paragraphs blocked. Remember to leave a line of clear space between the paragraphs. Compare them with the indented paragraphs. Which do you prefer?

I am taking great pride in my typing progress. Each day my skill grows and I am working more efficiently.
// Since so many jobs require typing I am preparing myself for a satisfying career.

1-minute timings

The following paragraphs will help you to get off a speed, control or fluency plateau. Start with the first 25 word paragraph and type it within one minute with complete keyboard control. If you make an error, type a line of that word, then do the timing again. When you have typed both 25 word paragraphs without error, go on to the 30 word paragraphs. Set the left margin at 10 and copy line for line.

25 words

a If you work to learn to type well, you will find that your skill grows each day through care for detail and a serious attitude.

b We wish to thank you for the interest you have shown in our company and have added your name to our complimentary mailing list.

30 words

a Taking care with your work does not mean that it need be boring; it just means that you take pride in knowing that each and every thing you do is right.

b In reply to your inquiry, your letter has been passed to the accounts department. You can expect to hear from the supervisor in the very near future.

35 words

a Nearly all of us like to produce work of a high standard and we strive to do our best in everything we do. For some, trying to achieve a perfect result is almost second nature.

b Our sales division is able to announce a ten per cent increase this quarter over the same period last year. We believe this to be the direct result of the new promotional policy.

40 words

a To be serious about your work will give you lasting pleasure in a job well done. You can be proud of your finished work because it should be truly attractive as it will be correct in every possible way.

b We would like to invite you to the grand opening of our new branch and enclose two tickets. Should you require more, please telephone our publicity department who will be only too pleased to send these.

Type these paragraphs experimenting with different sizes of paper, margin settings, aspects (landscape or portrait) and line spacing. Correct any errors you find in them. Produce each as a finished copy by correcting any errors you make.

TASK 1

Good techniques are built from day to day and form the basis of high speed in office tasks.// Work diligently to perfect your skills while maintaining good posture at all times.
Be aware of the value of daily practice.

TASK 2

My winter clothes seem to be in my closet all year round. I find boots when i'm looking for a sandals and a straw hat when there is a snow storme. there must be a better way to handle the weather.

TASK 3

Neatness counts. All the work your work Be should of the highest quality, in order to present you company in the best possible light. // Never settle for inferior workmanship. "Good enough" is never good enough.)
Excellence is always in style.

3-minute timings

You now move on to longer speed passages. The time shown in brackets is the time for which you should time yourself. Type through the passage until the time is up.

(3 minutes)

Do you have a pet? My friend Dianna has   8
a rather stupid collie she calls George.   16
George is beautiful but dense. He is so   24
stupid that one day he had nine puppies.   32

Mary had a pet, too. It was a lamb only   40
we never knew its name. It turned up at   48
school that day; Mary said she had tried   56
to send it home, but it followed her all   64
the time. It ate our botanical display,   72
then the geranium the teacher kept there   80
on her desk.   82

(3 minutes)

There are, of course, many kinds of pets   8
that people keep. They are not all such   16
stupid creatures as George nor as poorly   24
mannered as that lamb.   28

One of our neighbours has a snake. I do   36
not know what kind of snake it is but it   44
is big, about twenty feet long. It does   52
not make any noise and is very friendly.   60
One day I went to borrow a cup of sugar,   68
and that quiet, friendly snake had begun   76
to make friends with me before I had any   84
idea he lived there.   88

I now find that it has made many friends   96
besides me, all in the same quiet way.   104

All of us new friends had a meeting soon   112
after and it was decided that, no matter   120
how much we enjoyed peace and quiet, the   128
snake would wear a bell.   133

....1....2....3....4....5....6....7....8

Word division

To maintain a fairly even right-hand margin, it is sometimes necessary to divide a word and put part of it on the next line, although the trend now is to avoid breaking a word if possible.

Use a hyphen on the first line only and break the word between syllables as it is pronounced. Some words can be broken in more than one place, for example, con/ver/sa/tion. There should be at least 3 letters of the word on each line.

In general:

- Words with double consonants are divided *between* the consonants unless the root word ends in a double consonant. Dipping is divided dip-ping, but calling is call-ing.
- A hyphenated word is divided *only at the hyphen* (over-reacting) and a composite word *between* its parts (band-wagon).
- Words of one syllable (through), numbers (375.2), abbreviations (P & O), very short words (idea), and the last word on a page or in a paragraph are *never* divided.

TASK 1

Where would you divide the words below? Type the list showing the hyphen in each word, but only if the word can be divided.

```
temporary       bellringer
admiration      fiery
local           dial
wrapping        indefinitely
obnoxious       twenty-five
should          complicated
telling         delicacy
school          embellishment
```

TASK 2

Type the following paragraph on A5 paper, either landscape or portrait. Make your own decisions regarding line spacing and margins.

As you gain experience in typing, you will find it easier to judge the most effective placement on the page. You will be able to turn out expert quality work more and more quickly. Set a high standard for all work that you do.

5-minute timings

Use A4 paper. Set margins at 5 and 75.

(5 minutes)

Consider posture. To sit correctly at the keyboard, position both	13
feet flat on the floor and lean slightly forward, keeping your back	26
straight. Keep your elbows close to your body. Your neck should be	39
straight, too; do not allow your head to droop.	49

Always use correct fingering. You must not ever let yourself form	62
bad habits because they are so very hard to get rid of. In the same	76
way, good habits are just as difficult to break and are, therefore,	89
an aid to efficient typing. Form these good habits very carefully.	103

Never rest your hands on the keyboard. In fact, you should only touch	117
the key which is being struck. Let the other fingers hover or float	131
just barely above the keys but do not actually touch them. Letting go	145
of the keys, if you have not yet done so, will bring quick results.	158

(5 minutes)

Keep your hands as quiet as you can when you type. They should be	13
practically motionless; all the action should be in the fingers. By	27
typing in this way, you are using the fast muscles in the palm of the	41
hand instead of the slow ones on the back. Raising and lowering your	55
fingers uses the slow muscles and requires more than twice the effort.	69

If you are doing a difficult piece of work and it is needed at once,	83
do not rush. You will finish faster if you slow down instead, and	96
concentrate closely on the work itself. Then you will do it right	109
the first time. The techniques that you built so carefully will make	123
the typing of every task easier if you will allow your fingers to do	137
their work automatically, just the way you taught them. Trust them.	151

....1....2....3....4....5....6....7....8....9...10...11...12...13...14

Borders; margins

Borders

Some work, eg notices and menus, needs to be placed in the centre of the page so there is an even border all around it. We will learn how to do this later.

Margins

For most general office work, eg letters, memos, forms, the border is usually one inch on all sides. This is achieved by setting the margins.

Setting margins

Set each margin the same distance from the edge of the paper. If the left margin is 10, the right margin will be 10 spaces from the right edge of the paper.

For example, A4 portrait is 82 spaces pica, so the left margin will be at 10 and the right 82−10=72.

For elite, with 100 spaces A4 portrait, the settings will be 12 and 88 (100−12).

TASK 1

Calculate the following margins.

Paper	Aspect	Type	Line length	Left margin	Right margin
A4	Portrait	Pica	82	15	?
A5	Landscape	Elite	100	?	76

TASK 2

Practise setting the following margins:

left 10, right 10
left 20, right 20

Line-end bell

The bell on your machine will ring somewhere between 4 and 9 spaces before you reach the right margin. Each machine is different so you should check *each* machine you use. This will help keep your margin even, as you will see whether another word will fit on the line.

TASK 3

Type the following paragraph on A5 paper (portrait) using margins of 10 and 49 pica or 15 and 55 elite. Use single or double spacing.

```
Handle your work with care.  Treat it
with the respect it deserves.  When you
produce a high quality piece of work, be
sure not to wrinkle, smudge or smear it.
Let it represent you and your company in
the best possible light.
```

TASK 4

Type the same paragraph on A5 paper (landscape) using margins of 1½ inches pica or 2 inches elite. Use single or double spacing.

Practise letters confused

The following drills will help you to correct the substitution of one letter for another. From the column on the left, choose each pair of letters which you tend to confuse. Type the corresponding drill 3 times.

A/E are sea bean ear ashes rather shade ache
A/S sad sassy assist was sham ages bask wash

B/V bevy vibrate viable believe brave verbal

C/V clover victory vacant evict carve vector

D/E deed eddy red den shed deduct model idea
D/F fad deaf doff fiddle fodder duffle faded
D/K kid kudo duke dunked deck dusk skid dirk
D/S said shed speed dossier suds dust sudden

E/I heir their believe fire file epic relief
E/R red error cheer reel arrear tree premier
E/W crew we were ewer tweet woven flew where

F/G fig flag gruff foggy graft frugal fridge

G/H high hog chug thug ghost hang right gash
G/T night get tag goat tang great gutter got

I/O onion join oil iron action solid idolise
I/U ruin dubious cautious luxurious luscious

K/L talk kilt lake look link kill folk leaky

L/O log goal flog told yellow blossom lesson

M/N mind minnow numb minor nimble column men

O/P post polo open stop pro pillow prop port

R/T rot torn art try treat rust root rotated
R/U turn trust rush hurt our hurry round fur

S/W answer sweet sew was wish west stew wisp

T/Y city type tray toy yet tabby pretty trey

U/Y guy you fury duly fuzzy surly funny your

Paper sizes; paper aspects; use of paper

Paper sizes

International paper sizes (IPS) most commonly used in the office are A4 and A5. Note that the measurement system is based on a rectangle 1189 mm x 841 mm (A0) which maintains its proportions as it is progressively halved. Each size is one half the size of the one before. Therefore:

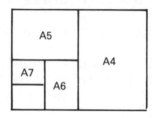

Sizes

A4 = 210 mm × 297 mm (approx 8¼" × 11¾")
A5 = 148 mm × 210 mm (approx 5⅞" × 8¼")
A6 = 105 mm × 148 mm (approx 4⅛" × 5⅞")
A7 = 78 mm × 105 mm (approx 3" × 4⅛")

Paper aspects

Instructions for the layout of work may include that the paper is to be used landscape or portrait. Fold a piece of A4 paper in half to make A5 size. Type your name at the top of the sheet both landscape and portrait, and label each with 'landscape' or 'portrait'.

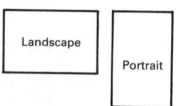

Use of paper

As you gain more experience you will find it easier to judge the most efficient size of paper for each task you do. The goal is to present the material clearly and attractively on the page. The paper should be large enough to prevent the work looking cramped but not so large that the work looks lost or paper has been wasted.

TASK

Type the following on a suitable size of paper. Use a 1 inch left margin and double spacing.

As your skill grows, you will find that the basic techniques you learned will become more and more important. We know that careful attention to detail builds high a level of skill.

Chaining drills

For each chain that is not fluent, type the corrective drill 3 times.

ab	able abet about aboard stab drab absence
ac	act acre traction grace placid practical
ad	ado admit adopt advised admire adventure
af	afar after aflame craft draft aft afghan
ag	age ago stag flag crag brag tragedy snag
ai	aim aid ail train flair stair braid aide
al	also alert alter praline alive alone alm
am	amp amble cram flame chamber amount amid
an	an clan scan trance angle change animate
ap	apt adapt staple drapery slap chap claps
ar	arc scar star charm argue ardent charged
as	as clasp blast quasi erase astute plasma
at	chat crater flat that what ate platen at
au	trauma auger audio frauds aural audition
av	avoid travel brave shave flavour average
aw	draw flaw slaw prawn brawl shawl awkward
ax	axe axle flax axiom climax klaxon praxis
ay	play tray shay quay fray flay prays clay
az	glazer azure crazy blazer shazam amazing
ba	band bard bask bash ball barn baste bank
be	be behind become between belt bend begin
bi	bird bind bike bible bison bill bias bin
bl	blue black blend blink blow block blonde
bo	box bore bond bold bob bomb body bog bop
br	brand brig brow brush break bring broken
bu	bus budge bunk burst butter bubble bumpy
by	by bye byte bygone bylaws bypass bystand
ca	can car cab cast call camp case cat cafe
ce	central cell cedar celery cereal certain
ch	chip chug church chair chop chose chapel
ci	circle circus cider cinema cigar cinders
ck	pack tuck pick sock peck lock rack trick
cl	clan clear club clip clam clog clue clot
co	cone cope core code cosy colt come cover
cr	cram cream crib cross cruel crypt cruise
cu	cup cub cut cull cube cushion cute curve
cy	cycle fancy cylinder cyst cynics cypress

(Contd)

Draft copy; correction signs

Draft copy

A *draft* (first copy) may need to be typed so that the author (or other person) can make amendments.

Correction signs

The symbols below are used to indicate corrections to draft copy.

Instructions to the typist or insertions can be enclosed in a balloon with an arrow.

#	leave a space	[or //	new paragraph
⌒	close up	λ	insert word(s) above or in balloon with arrow
⌐	run on		
⌒	transpose horizontally	.right.	stet (let it stand) or
⟲	transpose horizontally	⟨	in margin
⟨ ⟩	transpose vertically		

TASK

Type a correct copy of the following.

Use a 1 inch left margin and double spacing.

It was cold⟨#⟩and rainy that day I first not⌒iced

my boot was ⟨to⟩starting leak.

I stepped into⟨an⟩ankle-deep puddle that Friday

morning and before long I could feel my toes were

getting icy. The following day I priced new

boots and ~~decided~~ to have the old ones repaired.

da	dash dark daft dab date dally dare dance
de	dell dent desk deb depth dense defy deny
di	disk dip dish dill dial dine dire dimple
do	do doll does done dole dolt dome dot dog
dr	drag drew drip drop drum droop dream dry
du	due duty dust dull dunk dumb duel during
dy	dye ready trendy handy candy seedy gaudy

ea	each ear eat flea shear clean bread east
ec	eclair economy eclipse ecru elect eczema
ed	edit shed sped fled credo bred bled owed
ee	sheer sheep treetop free flee thee eerie
ei	either eider eight freight their sleight
el	elf elect elder elm elk elude shelf else
em	stem empty gremlin tremble ember embrace
en	enter ensued trendy then when end entire
ep	steps crept adept crepe slept epoch epic
er	ergo there where over ever erupt era erg
es	does escape presto escort escrow esquire
et	fret whet etude etch sketch eternal etna
eu	eulogy euphemisms euphoria eureka feudal
ev	evening clever ever eleven chevron every
ew	blew grew flew brew crew drew chew ewers
ex	excel extra flex exit exempt exist exult

fa	far fat fad fan fall fast fade fate faro
fe	fed fez fen fell fender felt defend fern
fi	file fish fin fir fill fig fit find fist
fl	fly flag flat flit flower flee flue fled
fo	for fog fob fold fore folk fond font fop
fr	fray free from fret frolic frugal friend
fu	fuzz full fury furl fuss future fund fur

ga	gate gather gall game gaze gasp gage gap
ge	gentle gesture get edge gene germ genius
gi	gill give girl gist gift giant gilt gird
gl	glad glue glib glut glow glen glee globe
gn	gnats signs deign gnarled gnu gnome gnaw
go	gone gold gobble go golf gopher governor
gr	grey gram grim grow grub grab grip angry
gu	guy gust gun gull gum gush gutter guitar
gy	edgy gymnasts gyp gyro gypsy dodgy pudgy

(Contd)

Making corrections

By now you may be aware of errors immediately they are typed. Correct these at once.

Use an eraser, correction paper or correction fluid if your machine is a manual.

For electric machines, correction paper or correction fluid will give good results. Some electric machines are fitted with a correction ribbon, which produces excellent results.

Electronic machines often have a display screen which allows the typist to make a correction before the letter is printed on the paper.

Erasing

Move the carriage to the right or left so any erasure dust will fall on the table rather than into the basket of keys.

Turn the cylinder down if the error is in the upper half of the page, or up if it is in the lower half. This will enable you to use the hard surface of the paper table or of the front frame to brace the paper.

Erase carefully and be certain not to rub a hole in the paper. Erase only enough to remove most of the ink. The new letter will cover any traces of the old one and you will lessen the risk of damaging the paper.

An electric machine usually produces an image too dark to be erased satisfactorily.

Correction paper

Hold a strip of correction paper with the chalky side facing the paper. Slip it behind the ribbon carrier and/or the card holder directly against the paper and strike the error again. Now the error will be covered exactly with white. Remove the correction paper, backspace and type the correct letter.

It is sometimes necessary to strike the correct letter a second time but do not do so immediately. First see if the correction blends with the rest of the line or paragraph. A slightly light letter is less noticeable than a slightly heavy one, so be sure a second stroke is required before you make it.

Correction fluid

Use this liquid sparingly. Dab it on the error with the tips of the bristles and use only enough to cover the error. Some brands are solvent based so be extremely careful not to inhale the fumes as they are toxic. Choose a water based product to avoid such a hazard. Solvent fumes are dangerous and their effects can be serious.

ha	have hart hall halt hand hasp hash happy
he	he help helmet hemp herd heft held hello
hi	high hire hill hilt hind hide hick hippo
ho	host horn hope honk hollow hobble hostel
hu	hull hurt hunt hunk hush hurry hulk hurl

ia	friar briar trial phial pliable initiate
ic	twice icing tropical icy italic friction
id	skid slid idle idiom idiot idol pride id
ie	friend client chief grief grievous brief
ig	ignite brigand brig frigid igloo ignoble
im	trim crimson imitate chimp climb climate
in	spin grin invest income shin skin inform
ip	grip trip clip flip ship drip slip chips
ir	iris spirit iron irked irate shire chirp
is	this thistle crisp isolate island chisel
it	quit grit item flit twit itch italic its

ja	jade jamb jazz jack jammed jagged jaguar
je	jest jelly jerk jetty jewel jester jerry
ji	jive jilt jitter jiggle jinx jigger jiff
jo	joke josh jolt jovial joss jolly jocular
ju	jury just jump jubilee juggle jumbo jute

ke	kelp kennel kettle kept kerosene ketchup
ki	kick kiln kilo kill kilt kitty kiss kite
kn	know knew knife knee knitted knot knobby

la	lacy last lash lake laddy lane lamb lamp
ld	held told weld cold bald gild build wild
le	less lend lent left legal lens lest levy
li	line liar like limp list lift light life
lk	talk walk chalk silk milk folk bulk sulk
lo	lose lost love local lock lobe lope lone
lt	wilt salt bolt colt vault melt kilt halt
lu	luck lure lush lump luke lute lull lucid
ly	only lyre duly rely wily easily polygram

ma	maze major male mare mace mate mall made
me	mess mesh melt mere merry mete menu meld
mi	mill mist miss milk mica might mile mice
mo	more most mole mock moss moth mode model
mp	lamp limp romp jump hemp camp lump stamp
mu	must mush mule muck muff mull music mute

(Contd)

42

Section 2 Principles of display

Proofreading; making corrections

All the finished work you produce from now on must meet a standard of **mailable copy** – copy which has no errors or discernible corrections.

A letter you type may be the first contact your employer has with the customer and your company will be judged by the quality of work you have produced.

Proofreading

To insure accuracy in your work, make it a rule never to remove the paper from the machine until you have read it carefully and made perfect corrections if any are to be made.

Read very carefully. Always read a detailed or complicated document aloud.

Double check numbers as these can be easily misread and mistyped. Spell names if they are unfamiliar, have alternate spellings or are similar to other names.

TASK 1

Find 5 errors in the second column, which should match the first column.

```
Roy Bell              Ray Bell
6164                  6164
17 April 1987         17 April 1978
Shelly Kent           Shelley Kent
213642                213642
412993                412293
27 June 1988          27 July 1988
```

Making corrections

Read the notes on p 48 and decide which method of correction you will use.

TASK 2

Type the words in the first column, then correct them as indicated in the second column.

```
bar                   ban
firm                  farm
fame                  same
```

na	name nave nape narrow nasty natural navy
nd	mind lend band pond fiend fund bond find
ne	nest neck never nephew neon nectar nexus
ni	nick nice ninny nine night nipper nibble
no	note none no noble nose norm nosy notice
nt	sent rant pint tent punt lent want meant
nu	null nudge numbers numerous nucleus numb
oa	oaf oath oar bloat oats oast cloak float
ob	obey blob obvious obese obstacle observe
oc	ocean ocarina ocelot octave oculist bloc
od	prod ode odour odious odometer shod trod
og	ogre ogle agog grog frog brogue fog clog
ol	old oleo olives stolen scold older olden
om	ominous bromide from promises omit omens
on	once only phone alone anon drone onerous
op	shop chop crop opera open flop opus stop
or	orbit order origin orange oral orchid or
os	close ostler those frost ostrich osmosis
ou	shout though brought cloud out our group
ov	over oven shove drove groves oval proven
ow	flow show stow grow blow slow clown brow
oy	boy joy coy oysters soy ploy tannoy troy
pa	past part park palm pale pace pack pager
pe	pert pelt pest pent peck pend penny perk
ph	phone photo phobia phase typhus physical
pi	pick pint pill pile pine pipe pike pinto
pl	play plan plot plea plum plus plug plant
po	pork pole pose pony poke port polar post
pr	pray prop prim pram prey prow prep prime
pu	push punt pure pull puce puma purl purse
qu	quad quit queue quiet quest quay quarter
ra	rash rant rack race rank rage rate rapid
rd	lord hard herd word bird horde ford card
re	rest rent rely rend reply regular relate
ri	rise ripe rile rind riot rival rite rich
rk	park dark lark lurk dirk work pork jerky
rl	hurl curl earl burl girl furl purl snarl
rn	corn darn learn fern turn horn burn torn
ro	rose rope role rode rote roll rota rover
rp	carp harp warp sharp chirpy twirp purple
rt	hart pert sort cart dirt curt dart spurt
ru	rude rush rust ruby runner rustle rudder

(Contd)

Double letter drills

Double letters

bb	babble rubble wobble nabbed ribbed lobby
dd	riddle huddle coddle wedded hidden daddy
ee	tree creep sleeve eerie speech eel sheep
ff	differ muffle coffee taffy baffle puffed
gg	logger bigger rugger haggle beggar foggy
ll	bill well tall full doll call mull silly
mm	summer gummy hammer hemmed dimmed simmer
nn	dinner funny penned fanned conned winner
oo	ooze brook spoon troop proof shoot sloop
pp	pepper happy topple copper supply ripple
rr	borrow carry burr mirror terror horrible
ss	lesson messy passed tussle missed tossed
tt	better litter matter putty totter cattle
zz	buzz fizz dazzle sizzle fuzz jazz muzzle

sa	sale sack sash salt safe sane save sally
sc	scan score scarf scoop disc scat scuttle
se	sell self sect send sent semi serf sense
sh	sham shag shy shed shop ship shut shrimp
si	sill silk sign sift sick side sigh silly
sk	ski skid skew skull skate skein sky skip
sl	slam sled slip slot slug slap slim slope
sm	smug smog smash smile smear smudge small
sn	snag snip sniff snug snow snap snub snob
so	sole sofa solo so soda sold soft somehow
sp	spy spin spun span spot sport spell sped
st	sty star stun stew stop stir store still
su	surf sure sulk sum suds sue super summer
sw	sway swag swim sweet switch swum swindle
sy	syrup system symbol easy cosy rosy daisy

ta	tack tape talk take talc tall tame table
te	test tell tether telephone terrace telex
th	the this that thus with then those there
ti	time tire tile tidy tick tide tilt tight
to	to toll tone tore torn towel toga topple
tr	try true trip tree tray troy trade trend
tu	turn tune tuft turf tube tuck tuba tutor
tw	two twin twice twain twill twelfth twist
ty	type tyre tyro tyrant typhus typist city

ue	clue flue true blue continue revenue sue

va	van vat vale vast vane vase vamp various
ve	vest vend vent very vessel vesper vetted
vi	vine vile visa vice vial visit vivid via
vo	vote vogue volley volume vocal volunteer

wa	want walk wash waft ward warn wallet was
we	we were went well west weld western welt
wh	who why what when where which whom while
wi	will wilt wide wile wind wine wise winch
wo	word work wove wore worn wolf woke woman
wr	write wrote wrist wreck wrap wrong wrung

ya	yarn yards yank yap yam yacht yakety yak
ye	yes yet yells yen yellow yegg yesterdays

ze	zest zero zen haze doze gaze zenith daze

Index

45